Out of Their League

Out
of
Their
League

by Dave Meggyesy

R

RAMPARTS PRESS, INC./BERKELEY, CALIFORNIA 1970

To Chris and Jennifer
May the vision of the new world be their reality.

Foreword

YOU MAY NOT KNOW IT, but you've probably seen me on television a few times during the last seven years or so—that is, if you're one of the 25 million Americans who zeroes in on pro football for several hours every fall weekend. I wasn't a glamour player, and the St. Louis Cardinals, where I played linebacker, wasn't a glamour team; but I was out there, along with a thousand or so other guys, most of them as anonymous as me.

But you won't see me out there again.

It's hard for me to count the reasons why. But I can begin by telling you about an image that is etched deep into my memory. The Cardinals were playing the Pittsburgh Steelers in St. Louis one rainy, cold Sunday afternoon. We were beating them easily and then, with a minute or so to go, they scored. I was playing end on the kickoff return team and my assignment was to swing more than halfway across field and block the third man from the kicker on the Pittsburgh team. I watched the flight of the ball as it went straight down the middle. Then I dropped back a few steps and began the sprint across field. My man must have thought someone had blown their blocking assignment or maybe it was because he was a rookie, but whatever the reason, he was making a bad mistake: running full speed and not looking to either side. I knew he didn't see me and I decided to take him low. I gathered all my force and hit him. As I did, I heard his knee explode in my ear, a jagged, tearing sound of muscles and ligaments separating. The next thing I knew, time was called and he was writhing in pain on the field. They carried him off on a stretcher and I felt sorry—but at the same time, I knew it was a tremendous block and that was what I got paid for.

During the rest of my years in the pros, this image would occasionally surface in my mind. This sort of thing happened all the time; it was part of a typical Sunday afternoon in big-time football. But the conditions that made me feel a confused joy at breaking up another man's body gradually became just one of many reasons why I decided to quit the game.

After playing the sport most of my life, I've come to see that football is one of the most dehumanizing experiences a person can face, and in this book I'm going to tell you what's really behind the video glitter of the game—the racism and fraud, the unbelievable brutality that affects mind as much as body. To me, it is no accident that Richard Nixon, the most repressive President in American history, is a football freak, and that the sport is rapidly becoming our version of bread and circuses.

Last spring, when I had already decided to get out of the game but hadn't yet made a formal announcement, I got a long-distance phone call from Cardinal head coach Charley Winner. He knew something was up and talked for more than two hours, repeatedly assuring me that I would be his starting right linebacker in 1970 and offering to forget my involvement in radical politics, a circumstance that had upset the Cardinals' organization in the past. A few days later I got a contract for $35,000 from St. Louis vice-president Billy Bidwell in the mail.

But they couldn't offer anything that would get me back into a football uniform and out onto the field.

To understand why, you've got to start at the beginning and understand what football does to the people who play it.

1

LOOKING BACK NOW, I realize many of the conditions that got me into a pro uniform and onto the football field were there from the very beginning.

I was born in Cleveland on November 1, 1941. My father had come to America from Hungary when he was nine years old and never got over the trauma of being an emigrant. He spent his youth farming strawberries in Louisiana and then came up to the big city to work as a tool and die maker. But by the time our family started to grow, he decided that urban life was becoming too dangerous. He had been doing some union organizing and things hadn't worked out very well. So when I was six, he moved me, my stepmother, older sister and four brothers to a 53 acre farm in Glenwillow, Ohio.

Though it was in the country, our house was hardly a rural paradise. My father had built it on weekends while we still lived in Cleveland. It was constructed with concrete blocks and had only one large room, in which all eight of us lived. The house had no running water. Toilet facilities were an outhouse equipped with a year-old Montgomery Ward catalogue and a slop bucket for inside the house. The bed which I shared with my three younger brothers consisted of an uncovered mattress and a couple of moth-eaten blankets.

Glenwillow, a town of 52 people, was controlled by Austin Powder Company, an explosives manufacturer. It was a sleepy American crossroads consisting of a general store, a few rundown houses for Austin employees, and an abandoned schoolhouse which served as a squatters' nest for local hillbillies.

My father was the sort of man who believed you were old enough to work when you were old enough to walk. All of us kids had jobs, even my three-year-old brother Joe. Mine was cow-watcher, an operation which allowed my father to avoid the expense and work of building fences. Carrying a piece of rye bread for my breakfast, I'd take the cows out to pasture at 7:00, keep watch over them until noon, then bring them back, water them down and take them back out for the afternoon. Two or three times every summer, I'd fall asleep and the cows would head for the cornfield. I'd chase them out and frantically try to cover up the damage they had done. But there was no way to disguise two rows of chewed-up corn, so I'd spend the rest of the day in terror, waiting for my father to come home. Depending on how drunk he was and where he happened to catch me, I was beaten with anything from a razor strop to an ax handle.

My father was superstitious about many things, including left-handed people. He thought they were inherently inferior and stupid. Unfortunately, I was left-handed, and every time he spotted me using my left hand for writing or eating, I would get a beating.

The old man got me for just about anything I did wrong—with one exception. One hot and dry summer morning I was watching the cows. We were about a half mile over the hill from the house, and I was playing with a pack of matches trying to build a fire. The dry buffalo grass caught fire and was soon out of control. I knew there was no way I could explain, so I got the cows together and headed for the swampy woods next to the burning field. From this vantage point, I was able to watch the Volunteer Fire Department from nearby Solon and about a hundred onlookers, including the mayor of Glenwillow, gather to watch the fire. About three hours later, I nonchalantly walked out of the woods with my cows in tow, just as the mayor, especially nervous because the Austin Powder Company stored tons of explosives near our property, was screaming at my father in front of the crowd, "Goddamn it, Meggyesy, can't you take care of your fields? It cost us $250 to bring the fire department out to fight this goddamn bush fire." My old man tried to save face by accusing me of starting the fire, but luckily the fire chief came to my rescue by convincing him that the fire started accidently.

Living on the farm was a very rough, almost primitive existence, especially because of the old man's brutality and because of the work he made us do. Things didn't improve much when I started going to school in Solon, a town of 5,000 people within commuting distance of Cleveland. It had an elite comprised of people who commuted to their professional jobs in Cleveland and lived in small enclaves of homes in exclusive areas with names like Briar Hill and Sherbrook Park. Their sons and daughters gave the Solon school system a college preparatory flavor and made me feel like one of those poor, dumb Meggyesy kids fresh off their run-down farm. This feeling of inferiority stayed with me throughout high school, and I know it stayed with my brothers. One of our prime motivations was to escape this feeling by achieving something big.

My first organized athletic experience was competing in track at Solon in the seventh and eighth grades. I was one of the smallest kids in my class and the coach assigned me to the mile run. In the few meets I ran in, I was one of the few milers ever to get lapped. The coach told us it was as important to finish the race as it was to win. I took his advice seriously, even though on more than one occasion it meant the humiliation of fighting my way through officials and runners preparing for the next race on my way to the finish line.

I began to play football in my sophomore year of high school. Practice for the Solon Comets began August 20, a few weeks before school opened. The assistant coach in charge of the backs was one of those crew-cut, drill instructor types—a real fanatic, always yelling, screaming, blowing his whistle and giving orders. On my first day out for the team, I felt like a fifteen-year-old virgin kid going to a whorehouse for the first time. I didn't quite know what to do so I picked up cues from the more experienced guys.

I was doing jumping jacks in a leisurely way when this coach came over and began watching me. He didn't know my name, but he noticed the number on my jersey. "Hey there! You, number 63, get your ass moving!" he shouted. I was startled and pointed to my number, which I hadn't yet memorized. "Yes, you," he yelled. "Get your ass in gear if you want to make this football team." I began jumping furiously—and kept jumping in one way or another until I quit football 14 years later.

The most significant thing to me about football that first year was not playing the game itself but gaining the approval and respect of Head Coach Bob Vogt. Like the other kids, I would do anything on the football field that I thought would make him happy. I became a back because it was the best chance to make the team, but I only weighed 150 pounds and I wasn't very good. Still, I quickly gained the admiration of my teammates and Coach Vogt for my aggressive play. I was a real hustling fanatic once I stepped onto the football field. This was the first time I had ever received praise directly for anything I had done and I thrived on it. Football quickly became my life, and, in a pattern I was to see repeated time and again, the coach became a sort of substitute father. Vogt at times seemed to show a genuine concern, perhaps because he too had been poor and made it through college only with the help of a football scholarship. I remember driving with him once when he pointed out his boyhood home, a dilapidated old farmhouse much like my own. He didn't say anything except that he had lived there as a boy; but the implication was clear to me: football could be my ladder to a new life, and Coach Vogt would be the model for a new me.

I knew almost nothing about football but I did know I was playing for big stakes—my own survival. And, although I didn't develop any real football finesse until near the end of my junior year, right from the start my trademark was that I was an aggressive, hustling hitter.

I still remember my first scrimmage. I was so frantic to make the team and please Vogt that I couldn't think straight. The one play I remembered was a 44 dive where the linemen split guard and tackle and the halfback drove through. Near the end of the scrimmage, the quarterback called on me for a 44 dive five times in a row. I remember one of those five times vividly: I had gone about five yards past the line of scrimmage before I was hit by the line-backer; I carried him for five more yards when he grabbed hold of my helmet and ripped it off, but I spun loose and went for 15 more yards before finally going down. It was an excruciating pleasure, making that run. I looked over and noticed the varsity players just staring in amazement and pointing at me, and Coach Vogt nodding in approval.

I developed a style the coaches loved. We moved in an Oedipal lockstep: the more approval they gave me, the more fanatically I played. From an early age, I had learned to endure violence and brutality as simply a part of my life. But in football, the brutality became legitimate, a way of being accepted on the football field and off.

My fanatical approach had its limits, though. I didn't play much because I got so hyped up I often couldn't remember the plays. Our first game my sophomore year was against Cuyahoga Heights, a pretty rough bunch of kids from a steel town on the west side. They didn't have much finesse; they simply beat the shit out of their opponents. Russ Davis, our regular right halfback, was hurt, and Coach Vogt put me in the game. I freaked out, getting so excited I couldn't remember the plays except for my old standby, the 44 dive. I survived the first series because the quarterback stuck mainly to this play, but when he began to mix the plays up, it was all over. I was asking him in the huddle, "Where do I go on this one? What do I do?" He finally got pissed off and motioned to Coach Vogt, who quickly hustled me off the field.

Toward the end of my sophomore year I began to develop a little football ability to go with my kamikaze style of play. The last game of the year was against the Brecksville Bees. Many of the Brecksville players looked about 20 years old, and in their fancy red and orange uniforms they had most teams beaten before the game began. Even Coach Vogt didn't expect the game to be too close and—since it was the last game of the year—said he was going to take a good look at the sophomores. My good friend Bill Davidson, who had been a starting end all season although he was just a sophomore too, told me this was my big chance, that if I did well in the last game I would be assured a starting position the following year.

The Brecksville game was scheduled for Friday night, but by Tuesday I was all psyched up and ready to play. That Wednesday was Halloween, and down at the local drive-in restaurant I ran into some of the senior ball players who had a supply of firecrackers and Roman candles. One of them had a truck and they asked me if I wanted to come along with them to have some fun. I hopped in the back of the truck and we drove up to the expensive Briar Hill section. We cut loose with a barrage of Roman candles and firecrackers directed at everything from mailboxes to the sprawling split-level houses.

We made a clean escape from Briar Hill and decided that Mr. Smith, the principal of Solon High School, would be our next target. It was about 1:30 in the morning when we climbed to the crest of the hill overlooking his house with dozens of eggs stuffed in our jackets. We commenced firing them and kept it up for about ten minutes, becoming bolder and bolder. Finally we were running down the hill to get his house at close range. About five of us were in his back yard when he flipped on his floodlights. He began to yell, "Meggyesy, Clark, Keldorf, I know who you are." I was paralyzed with fright. Within seconds, three carloads of police pulled up. The few guys who hadn't come down the hill escaped, but those of us who were captured were forced to stay out there scrubbing down his house until five in the morning.

The next day we were called down to Mr. Smith's office, and when we arrived Coach Vogt was there too. They were both pissed off but for different reasons. Smith wanted to punish us, but felt hamstrung because we hadn't broken any school regulations and he wasn't enough of a bastard to press criminal charges. But he knew we had violated the 10 p.m. football curfew and that Vogt was a stickler about curfew violations. True to form, Vogt informed us that we were all banned from playing against Brecksville. I was really broken up and almost felt like begging Vogt to let me play. I felt his rejection; I had let him down. More acutely, I recognized the unlimited power those in control had, and I wanted to make sure they didn't get me again. From then on, I played it straight through the rest of high school.

Basketball practice began a week after the football season ended. I went out for the junior varsity team, which Bob Vogt also coached. As in football, I didn't have much finesse, but won a starting position on the basis of my brutal rebounding. I was the team's hatchet man, and the aggression expected of me on the football field spilled over to my play on the court. Once I remember coming down with a rebound and instinctively tucking it under my arm and running up court.

In the spring of my sophomore year I decided to leave Solon and go live with my uncle in Detroit. Things had really disintegrated at the farm. My older brother had gone into the Navy and my sister had left for Cleveland to get married. The old man was hitting the bottle heavily and he and my stepmother were about to get a divorce. I went to Coach Vogt for advice. We had a long talk in his office. He strongly suggested I stay in Solon since I had already established myself as an athlete, and told me I had shown enough promise as a sophomore to have a good chance of winning a college football scholarship in my senior year. As I was leaving his office he told me Mark Weber, the star of that year's team and a player he knew I greatly admired, had received a football scholarship to Syracuse and suggested I keep that in mind.

My friend and teammate, Bill Davidson, had also heard of my plans to move to Detroit, and, unknown to me, had approached his parents about the possibility of my moving in with them. Bill's father was an executive with General Electric and they lived in a secluded redwood ranch house in Briar Hill, the most exclusive residential section in Solon. I was to spend a week living with the Davidsons on a trial basis to see how we would get along. After one of Mrs. Davidson's meals, I was determined to be on my best behavior! Living there would be like mov-

ing from a pigpen to a palace. At the end of the week,
they told me I could move in if it was all right with my
parents. The old man had no objections, so I gathered all
my belongings in a brown paper bag, said goodbye to my
brothers, and left home.

2

WHEN I WENT OUT for football practice the summer before my junior year, Coach Vogt switched me to tackle. I had grown a lot that summer but I'd also lost some of my speed and coordination. I had been living with the Davidsons for about three months by the time practice started, which meant eating three full meals a day for the first time in my life. Besides the regular meals, Bill and I were allowed to take food from the refrigerator whenever we were hungry. The first few times I did this, I would glance over my shoulder to see if anyone was watching, remembering the beatings I got from my father for sneaking a hot dog or two from the ice box at home.

The Davidsons took other pressures off me as well. They continually stressed that Bill and I should question things and be free to talk about our ideas within the family. Compared to anything I'd known before, they provided a free environment where I could begin to express myself. In fact I couldn't believe that they were for real at first, and I remember fantasizing that they were actually Communist agents out to diabolically control my mind. But I finally got over my suspicions and came to accept and return their love and trust.

Still, adjusting to life at Briar Hill put me through a lot of mental changes. Not long after I moved in, Mrs. Davidson took me to a men's store in Cleveland and outfitted me in the style of the day—button-down shirts, V-neck sweaters, khaki pants, and loafers. This was quite a change from my J.C. Penney blue jeans and Montgomery Ward flannel shirts, and it confused the students at Solon: the poor, dumb Meggyesy kid was now dressing with class and sharing a Ford convertible with Bill Davidson.

I was a marginal man, as I would be for years to come, although the reasons changed. My new home and Ivy League clothes separated me from my old circle of friends, yet I wasn't fully accepted by the class-conscious Briar Hill kids. Even later when I developed into the star football player of Solon High, these people never accepted me as an equal, except on the athletic field.

I played tackle for most of my junior year and was having a rather unspectacular season until the next to last game of the season against Cuyahoga Heights. We were down by two points going into the fourth quarter. Coach Vogt called quarterback Russ Keldorf and myself over to the sideline and told us he wanted me to switch to halfback. Since I was unfamiliar with the plays, Keldorf was instructed to stick to three basic plays, two of which had me carrying the ball. The field was muddy from a constant drizzle and when I went in at halfback we began to move for the first time that evening. With four minutes to go, we had worked down the field twice, only to have them stop us inside their twenty. Keldorf was calling my old standby, the 44 dive, most of the time, and I was picking up eight to ten yards at a crack, but we just couldn't get the ball into the end zone. With three minutes and 50 seconds to go, we began our last drive on our own 35 yard line. I carried the ball 12 times in a row and with 45 seconds to go we had first and goal to go on their three yard line. A touchdown would mean victory. By this time, though, the Cuyahoga Heights defense was keying on me, and the yardage was getting tough. Coach Vogt tried to be tricky, and sent in a play calling for a sweep by our other half-back. He was thrown for a yard loss. On second down another play came in from the bench—a pass to our tight end. It was nearly intercepted and fell incomplete. On third down, Vogt sent in my 44 dive. The hole was closed but I blasted my way down to the one yard line. I came back to the huddle really beat. It was fourth down with six seconds left on the clock. Vogt once again called for the 44 dive. Cuyahoga Heights had four men stacked in the hole and I could see them waiting for me. On the snap, instead of leveling my head and blasting in there, I hesitated, looked for an opening and attempted to pick my way through the pile. They nailed my ass and we lost the game.

I remember sitting by myself in a corner of the locker room, crying my head off. I felt it was my fault that we had lost the game. But even worse, I felt I had let Coach Vogt down. On my way into the locker room I had over-heard him say to one of his assistants, "If he had hit in

there like he did on third down, instead of trying to pussy-
foot it over, he would have made it."

Looking back, the Cuyahoga Heights game was one
of the many times in my football career when I saw clearly
how corrupt the whole thing was and could have turned
back—but decided to press on for reasons I didn't understand. I was really broken up, and I hoped Coach Vogt
would say something to lessen my guilt. Instead he ignored me. Finally, I started to get angry. I thought,
"Christ, I put out all this energy for a game and if it
wasn't for me, it wouldn't even have been close." It was
clear that Coach Vogt's prime concern was in winning
football games and that he was concerned about his players only to the extent that they could contribute to that. He
had been telling me for two years how much he cared
about me as a person and I had believed him; but after I
went all out to win a game and just barely failed, Vogt
had no words for me. I never completely believed in
coaches after that, although I wasn't quite able to step
outside the father-son relationship that is football's cor-
nerstone.

I also played basketball and ran track my junior year,
but my participation in these sports was rather uneventful.
I once again played the hatchetman role in basketball and
ran the sprints and anchored the mile relay in track. Track
was the most painful sport I have ever participated in. Our
track coach had been a distance man in college, and he
made the entire team, including sprinters, train like milers.
Despite this, I liked track because it was the one sport
where I got a chance to talk to athletes from other schools.
In football these same guys were the faceless enemy, but

in track we could lie around on the grass between events and rap. Track was a more natural sport—you could do what you had to do even though you were friendly with members of the other team.

Late in the spring just before school let out, I was elected football captain for the upcoming season. This made me feel directly responsible for the success of the team. Bill Davidson and I began serious training in July, a month before pre-season practice officially began. As captain, I wanted to build great *esprit de corps* among the players. In August, I had a party for the ball players at the Davidsons' to get the team together. We talked about what we had to do if we were going to be a winner that season. Our goal was the county championship.

By the time practice started on August 20, I weighed 195 pounds and had developed sprinter's speed. The first day of practice Coach Vogt put me at fullback, and in pre-season scrimmages I was just about unstoppable. I set a goal for myself to score at least one touchdown a game. The first game was against North Royalton. Through the first three quarters, I was picking up good yardage on quick hitters. I hit them really hard and quickly cleared the line of scrimmage. Once beyond the line I would smash straight ahead or slide to the outside and go down the sideline. I had watched Jim Brown play and was trying to imitate his running style.

But despite all the yardage I had gained I hadn't been able to break loose for a touchdown. Then, early in the fourth quarter, the quarterback called a 32 trap. I shot through the hole, broke the linebacker's tackle and had only the safety between me and a touchdown. I had my balance and was running full speed. Just as the safety ducked his head to get me, I caught him with a forearm and ran over him for a 72 yard touchdown.

The season was off to a great start. We had won, and I had a good game. The next Monday, Coach Vogt called me out of study hall to talk with me. Standing in the hallway, he began to lay this rap on me about girls, school, and football. "There are three things a person can do when he is in high school," he began. "He can play football, he can study to keep his average up, or he can go out with girls. And you can't do more than two of these things well." I had never seen things this way and he could see the puzzled look on my face. He went on to tell me there was a "certain girl" in the school who had "destroyed" one of our top players the year before. I had just begun going out with her (she was one of Solon's cheerleaders and the toughest-looking girl in the school). In one way Coach Vogt and I had similar concerns: we were both worried about my getting together with this certain girl.

He also mentioned that I had a good future in football, and added that if I continued like I did in the first game I might get a scholarship to Syracuse, whose chief scout, Bill Bell, had picked up two former Solon High players: Roger Davis and Mark Weber. Vogt even told me a solid recommendation from him would guarantee me a scholarship to Syracuse. The implication was clear: if I played ball with Coach Vogt and not with this girl, I would be sure to get a scholarship to Syracuse. I complied.

This brief encounter was a good metaphor for the whole high school football ethic. The coach was not only concerned with football; consciously or unconsciously, he was trying to instill in us a particular view of the world. We were made to feel that, because we were football players, we were somehow superior. Vogt tried to get us to see ourselves as the "good people" in the school as opposed to the "bad people"—those who weren't submitting themselves to the system. He felt that as you became a better athlete you became a better person. Football represents the core values of the status quo, and coaches and school administrators want players to win adherents to these values, not only on the football field but also in their private lives.

There was always an attempt to make sure everyone subscribed to the suburban middle-class values dominant in the school. For instance, the informal uniform of Solon High for boys was khaki pants, button-down shirts, and V-neck sweaters, and anyone who had some stake in status was expected to conform to this code. I had this black knit sweater that I wore occasionally. It fit kind of tight and I remember some of the younger female teachers would look me over pretty good. But every time I wore this sweater there were always whispers, whispers from Vogt and from other teachers. Nothing was ever said outright, but after a while I stopped wearing it.

As team captain, it was my responsibility to help get the guys psyched up for each game. Every Thursday afternoon, after the last practice session before the game, the team would meet on the practice field without the coaches. I'd give an impassioned speech on how we had to win the game for the school, Coach Vogt, and the whole coaching staff. I'd put a lot of stress on team pride, individual pride, and the tradition of good football at Solon High. I would point out that many people would be watching us and we had to show we were a good football team and that we weren't quitters. Then I'd go on to talk about one or two good players from the team we would face in Friday night's game and what strategy we should use to handle them. I'd stress to them how we had to obliterate everything from our minds except football between now and game time, so we would be mentally ready for the game. Finally, I would kneel down and the team would gather around me. We would all put our hands together. Then I'd say, "We're going to get them," and they'd scream, "Yeah." Then I'd holler, "OK, let's go get them," and we'd break out and head for the locker room feeling psyched up for the game.

Our games started at eight o'clock. At four-thirty, Bill Davidson and I would have our pre-game meal. We always ate the exact same thing: a cup of tea with four spoonfuls of sugar and some mashed up broiled hamburger on a piece of toast. Dick Clark's rock and roll show was always on at this time, so we would watch it on the tube and hope he played a lot of heavy rock music to help us get psyched up. A little after six we'd leave for a special service at the Solon Presbyterian Church. Rev. Bill Drake, a former college athlete, would give a short inspirational talk and lead us in prayer. We'd leave the church ready for a battle that by that time seemed like the final contest between good and evil.

At the stadium, we'd get our ankles taped, put on our uniforms, and then lie around the locker room looking very solemn. Except for Coach Vogt's pep talk the locker room resembled a funeral parlor. We all felt somewhat uncomfortable and were anxious to get out of it. We had to walk about 60 yards from the locker room to the big chain link fence surrounding the playing field as the fans were flowing in. At the gate to the field the guys would gather around me and I'd say, "We're really going to win tonight, it's a crucial game. I know everybody is ready to play." And then I'd say "We're going to get them," and they'd answer "Yeah!" We'd repeat this four or five times until we really got ourselves going and then, boom, the gate would fly open, we'd burst through and run single file around the field.

Since we only had 26 guys we would really spread ourselves out when doing our pre-game lap around the field. I remember the time we were playing Mayfield High School, which came to Solon with a herd of about 60 guys. They looked like an army when they paraded around the field and did their calisthenics. I remember saying to myself while warming up, "I don't know about this game." I was really swallowing it. It was near the end of the season, and I was being touted as the best fullback in the county. They kicked off, and on the first play from scrimmage I went through on a quick hitter off tackle. I was met at the line of scrimmage by their linebacker and their tackle Darryl Sanders, who later starred at Ohio State and with the Detroit Lions. They really put it to me, and as they were getting up the linebacker said, "Fucking Meggyesy, you're not so tough." I knew then it was going to be a long night. I managed to gain over 100 yards, but for the first time in my life I began to experience fear on the playing field. The fears kept creeping in and for a while I could hardly control them. I began to question the brutality of the game—these guys on the other side of the line were obviously trying to smash the hell out of me. (In some ways I found the hitting in high school more painful than in the pros. By the time I got to the pros, even though the hitting was more violent, it usually didn't hurt as much because I had learned how to take the blow.)

But I learned a lot more about pain the first time I ever played with a serious injury. That was the Warrensville game my senior year. Warrensville was always a tough team and beat us more than we beat them. On the Tuesday before the game, Coach Vogt had us doing this drill we called "ground-hogging." Two players would get down on their hands and knees facing each other—you could only use your head and had to keep your hands and knees on the ground. The object of the drill was to butt the other player on his back, and the lower you got to the ground the better leverage you had for tipping him over. During this drill I injured my neck so badly that the next morning I couldn't move my head—it was stuck over to one side. I went to the doctor that afternoon and he diagnosed it as a "wry neck." He told me not to practice for the rest of the week and to come back on Friday. My neck had not improved by Friday morning, but when Coach Vogt saw me at school, he said he hoped I would be ready for the game that night. I was anxious to play, too, for it was a big game and I had never missed a game because of an injury.

I went to the doctor Friday afternoon before the game. He stuck a long needle into the big muscle knot in my neck. When he tried to pull the needle out, the muscle spasmed. The needle broke from the base of the syringe and I was left with it sticking in my neck. The doctor took a pair of pliers out of the drawer and pulled it out. Mrs. Davidson had brought me to the office, and when she saw this, she turned very pale and I thought she was going to pass out. I was so spaced out about playing, though, it didn't matter at all to me. I didn't realize it, but he was shooting me up with Novocaine for the game. He assured me everything would be all right, and sure enough much of the pain was gone by the time I left his office. I still couldn't move my neck, but I was happy it didn't hurt any more.

Coach Vogt used me only on third downs during the first half of the game. Our offensive series went something like this: we would make just about no yardage on the first two downs. Vogt would send me in at fullback. We'd hit a quick trap and I'd go for about ten yards. We'd have a first down and the Coach would pull me out. The team would run two more plays, gain little or no yardage, and Vogt would shoot me back in. I would once again run a quick trap over the middle and gain another ten yards for a first down.

When we came out for the second half we were down by 14 points, and Vogt began putting me in on second down situations and keeping me in for two or three plays. By the fourth quarter we were still behind, and Vogt now had me on the field for just about all the offensive plays. We moved the ball well and scored a few touchdowns. However, we couldn't contain them at all on defense and we lost the game.

When the numbness wore off after the game, my head felt like it was on backwards. But even though the pain in

my neck kept getting worse as the drug wore off, I was
required to go to the post-game party with all of the other
players. Coach Vogt started these gatherings for both
teams in my junior year. They were hosted by the owner
of a local restaurant, and most of us made an appearance
only because we were required to. It seemed stupid; Vogt
had been getting us psyched up all week to beat the shit
out of our opponents, and then he expected us to sit down
and be friendly over Cokes and hotdogs after we battled
them for two hours on the playing field.

The business of setting up a dividing line between us
and our opponents went on the whole week before a
game. Vogt would call Chagrin Falls, our big rival, "the
boys from across the river," and Mayfield was a team of
"dumb but tough Wops." And at the beginning of the
game I would give my "We've got to get them, we've got
to get them" speech. We were really fired up and felt we
were going to annihilate "them." I particularly didn't want
to see their faces, because the more anonymous they were
the better it was for me—and I'm sure most of the other
ball players felt the same way: they were a faceless enemy
we had to meet.

We finished my last high school season with one of
the best records Solon had had in some time. I was the
league's leading rusher and top scorer and was selected to
the all-county all-star team at fullback. That winter Bill
Bell, an assistant football coach at Syracuse University,
came down and looked me over while I was playing basketball. He had a long meeting with Coach Vogt during which
he viewed some of our game films. That night the Davidsons had Bell out for dinner. I had been taught to be

humble, never to say, "I was this," or "I was good" but always "It was my team that was good, without my team I would have been nothing." So when Bell was there, I really humble-pied it. I remember telling him, "I would really like to go to Syracuse; I hope I might be able to contribute to your fine football program." Bell assured me Syracuse was definitely interested in me and that I would be hearing from them before too long.

The weekend after Bell's visit, Miami of Ohio brought me down on a recruiting visit. While I was there it was arranged for me to play basketball with some of the football players. Miami football coaches came out of their offices to watch us. When football players play basketball, the game is more like a street brawl. So I got in there and was pretty rough. The coaches liked what they saw and offered me a scholarship.

Syracuse heard of my visit to Miami and flew me up there almost immediately. It was winter and freezing cold. Mark Weber, my old teammate at Solon, met me at the airport with Coach Bell. We drove back to the University where I was introduced to Ben Schwartzwalder, the head football coach. Our meeting lasted about one minute. Schwartzwalder told me how he had heard a lot of good things about me and said he hoped I would be joining his program. I had dinner with Mark and some of the other football players, and then Mark took me out to the Clover Club. The Clover Club was in a rough section of town and was a favorite hangout for Syracuse football players. There was always a lot of action there. Mark introduced me to this real tough college chick. We really hit it off and before long we had retired to the back seat of Mark's car in the parking lot. It was about 20 degrees and snowing like crazy and I nearly froze my ass off.

When I returned to Solon, I phoned John Pont, the head football coach at Miami, and told him I'd decided on Syracuse. "Hey, wait a minute, are you sure?" he asked me. "Lookit, I'll send you some tee shirts, do you want some Miami tee shirts?" I told him, "No, don't bother, I really have decided, it would be awfully nice of you, but I really don't want to bother you. My decision is final." He said to let him know if I changed my mind and that he would send the tee shirts anyway.

After this bidding seemed to be over, during the spring of my senior year, I began to give a lot of speeches on the character-building value of athletics. I still remember one solemn talk I gave to the entire student body at Solon High about how athletics had made me what I am—stressing how one could get ahead through hard work. I talked about the great respect I had for the coach and the principal, and how important these men had been in my life. I praised the athletic department at Solon High, because they were instrumental in getting me a scholarship to Syracuse. I had begun to think and talk like a patriotic Rotarian.

Shortly after I graduated from high school I went down to visit two cousins in Baton Rouge, Louisiana. One of them had played defensive end for the Chinese Bandits on the Louisiana State University National Champion team of 1958. His younger brother, Gary, who was entering LSU in the fall, was a high school All American. My cousins' house was near the LSU campus and we spent a lot of time during my visit hanging around with some of the big-name LSU jocks like Billy Cannon and Warren Rabb. Gary and I worked out every day with many of the LSU football players, doing a lot of calisthenics and running. One morning we were working out by Tiger Stadium when Head Coach Paul Dietzel and a few of his assistants wandered by. They asked some of the players who I was and that afternoon they called Gary's home and offered me a scholarship. Though I was still planning on going to Syracuse, I was very interested in LSU. They were the National Champions and Baton Rouge was the most football crazy town I had ever seen. The people were falling all over their feet to be with or to know football players. I told Dietzel I'd accept his offer, and he told me the Davidsons' signature on a letter of intent would be needed before I could be officially awarded a scholarship. He tried hard to get me to handle the whole thing by mail, and Gary's parents also wanted me to stay in Baton Rouge, but the Davidsons insisted I come home and talk the whole matter over with them.

By the time I got home I was really in a turmoil. I called Coach Bell at Syracuse to tell him I had decided to go to LSU. He asked me how I could do such a thing to him after he had personally recruited me. The old feeling of guilt crept over me. Within five minutes after I stopped talking with Bell, Ben Schwartzwalder called. As usual, he did not waste any words. "Boy, you fly up here immediately. We'll pay for the plane," he told me, "just get up here by tomorrow." No sooner had Schwartzwalder hung up than I received a call from Col. Byrne, head of the Air Force ROTC program at Syracuse. The Colonel said he had just talked with Ben Schwartzwalder and was calling because he had learned I was interested in becoming a jet pilot. He personally assured me I would be able to go through the Air Force ROTC program and could enter flight school when I graduated from college.

I arrived in Syracuse the next day and was met at the airport by Jim Shreve, the freshman coach. He took me to my room at the Hotel Syracuse and then left, saying he would return with Coach Bell at six o'clock for dinner. I waited around by myself for about two hours feeling anxious as hell. About six Bell called to tell me they were waiting for me in the hotel dining room. I walked down and saw what seemed to me to be the entire Syracuse coaching staff sitting there with one empty chair reserved for me. Schwartzwalder, the head coach, whom I had met only briefly on my recruiting trip to Syracuse, was at the head of the table. Seated around him were Bell, Shreve, and Joe Szombathy, the end coach who was there to play on my ethnic sensibilities because he too was of Hungarian descent. The chair reserved for me was directly across from Ben and I couldn't escape his gaze. Ben talks in this raspy, gravelly voice. His head is usually lowered and he peers at you over the top of his glasses. Bill Bell sat there, asking every few minutes how I could do this to him. He looked hurt. The waitress came over to take our order, but Ben shooed her away. She must have known I was starved, for she came back about every ten minutes. Ben never took his eyes off me, never stopped talking. "Boy, we had great plans for you," Ben would say, and Szombathy or Shreve would second him. Ben went on to say how Mark Weber and Roger Davis, two other football players from Solon High, were doing a great job for him. They really came on heavy against LSU. Shreve told me, "Dave, if you told us you wanted to go to Notre Dame, or some other fine school, we wouldn't say anything. But we would be doing you an injustice if we didn't object to your going to LSU." Even though the public schools I had gone to in Ohio were always all white, they made a big point of telling me "There will be no colored students at LSU." After a while they began to focus on how Syracuse was a small school with a limited number of scholarships, and how it would be impossible for them to give my scholarship to someone else at this late date. I finally agreed to go to Syracuse. They were all smiles and assured me how happy I would be. Then Ben finally allowed the waitress to come over and take our orders.

The next morning Coach Bell picked me up at the hotel to take me to the airport for my flight back to Ohio. Col. Byrne, the Air Force ROTC commander whom I had talked to briefly on the phone, was with him in the car. When we arrived at the Syracuse airport, Bell drove over to the National Guard hanger, and Col. Byrne got out to speak with some of the Guardsmen stationed there. He asked me if I would like to sit in a jet, so I climbed up, and he spent a few minutes explaining the controls. Once I was back in Solon, Coach Bell would call me every week to see how I was doing and to tell me how personally pleased he was that I was going to Syracuse. He assured me he would do anything he could to make my four years at Syracuse as enjoyable as possible. I would always reassure him that I was coming to Syracuse, and thank him for the personal interest he had in me.

3

For incoming freshman football players, practice began at Syracuse on September 5th even though classes did not start for another two weeks. Bill Davidson was going to play on the freshman team at Colgate University and he also had to report for practice on the 5th. Since Colgate is located about forty miles east of Syracuse, Bill's father made arrangements for the two of us to take the 10 p.m. train out of Cleveland so we would arrive in Syracuse as the sun was rising the next morning. The metaphor was obvious: it was the dawning of a new day, and we were on the verge of a new career.

I arrived tired from a night made sleepless by excitement and anticipation over the beginning of college. After collecting my luggage I immediately telephoned Coach Bell who had insisted that I call him the minute I got into town so he could pick me up at the station and get me settled in the football living quarters. His phone rang for a very long time and I was just about ready to hang up when he answered. Our conversation went something like this: "Hello Coach Bell? This is Dave. I just arrived and I'm down at the train station." There was a long silence and I started to get a little nervous. "Do you realize what the hell time it is?" he growled. "Yes, Coach, it's about 6:20 in the morning." By this time he was really pissed and told me to meet him at the Syracuse Gym around 9 o'clock. Since I didn't know my way around town, I asked him how I should go about getting there. "I don't care," he responded; "just don't ever wake me up this early in the morning again." I wandered around the train station for a while and then took a cab to the university. It was a little after 7 a.m. and no one was around yet, so I walked over to Archibald Stadium behind the Gym. I still remember looking down into this concrete bowl with its 35,000 seats and wondering if I would ever really play there. I was excited and felt good about being at Syracuse. It was like a scene from Horatio Alger.

My freshman year, 1959, Syracuse had recruited the best group of football players they could find. Age didn't matter much, and the freshman team was split into two groups: the guys who couldn't vote, 17- and 18-year-olds; and guys ranging in age anywhere from 21 to 25. Our backfield was composed of two ex-marines, an army veteran and a 17-year-old quarterback, Bob Lelli, who tried ineffectually to be a field general and give orders to older men.

I was recruited by Syracuse as a fullback but was switched to center the first day of practice. I can still remember Coach Shreve saying casually, "Meggyesy, you're a center now, get over there with the linemen."

Later I learned that Syracuse always recruited a surplus of fullbacks and then made most of them into linemen. I was anxious to play football and didn't particularly care where I played. But I still remember thinking at the time it would have been nice if they could have let me know what their plans for me were.

The linemen, like the backs, included three or four guys in their early twenties. The rest of us were young kids just out of high school who found it strange to be playing with guys who had been through the Army. Most of them had a very casual attitude when it came to practice, but once the hitting began they were mean, rough players. During scrimmages there would often be several slugging matches. This was the first time I'd ever seen guys really break loose on each other. I was also amazed at the way coaches would say "Let them fight" and prevent other players from breaking it up.

We had two practice sessions a day for a week and didn't get our first break until freshman orientation day. It seemed like we had been at Syracuse for ages, and right from the start we didn't feel much fellowship with the other freshmen. When I saw them running around the quadrangle in their orange beanies, it hit me how different I was. On the one hand, I felt somewhat superior, but on the other hand they made me realize I was part of a select group of individuals brought there to play football, not to have a "normal" college experience.

The following day we had to register for courses. Syracuse had a special remedial program, ostensibly designed to help freshmen entering with academic deficiencies. But the coaching staff encouraged me and the other freshmen football players to enroll in this program because it lasted through the whole year and consisted of mainly "Mickey Mouse" courses requiring little work.

Joe Szombathy, the varsity end coach, was also in charge of the athletic tutoring program. He would take the freshmen football players' class cards and simply fill out the courses he wanted them to take. Szombathy not only enrolled most of them in the remedial program, but decided on their courses with one of the main criteria being whether or not they interfered with afternoon football practice. I had searched through the course catalogue for classes I wanted to take, then filled out my own course card and presented it to Szombathy. He was furious. "What the hell do you think you're doing, Meggyesy?" he shouted at me. "We want you to take these other courses so you'll be sure to be eligible. You can always take the other course next year." But I was conscious of not wanting to be identified as a stupid jock, and I refused to allow him to sway me. I simply wanted to take the courses other freshmen were required to take.

Jim Shreve, the frosh coach, had just been hired and was out to prove himself. He had been on one of Schwartzwalder's teams a few years before but never really played much. Guys with backgrounds like this usually become the truly hard coaches, and Shrieve proved to be almost fanatical. He luxuriated in the military discipline of the situation and worked us like animals. We had to hit every day and scrimmage every other day. I remember one afternoon when it was snowing so bad that Schwartzwalder had called off practice for the varsity, but Shreve had the freshmen out there working. Some of the varsity players just stood around in their street clothes watching us with disbelief.

We had our first and only scrimmage against the varsity a week before their opening game. This was the team that went on to an undefeated season and to win the National Championship with a victory over Texas in the Cotton Bowl. It was loaded with players like Ernie Davis, Art Baker, Roger Davis, Bruce Tarbox, Tom Gilberg and Fred Mautino, all of whom went on to win All American honors or play pro ball. With all the rumors of how great the varsity was, most of the frosh players were really anxious. I was scared but also excited about having the chance to test myself against proven college players.

It was much like college guys going against pros for the first time. When the scrimmage began, we held our own and even managed to get in some pretty good licks. I was playing linebacker and tackled Ernie Davis a couple of times behind the line of scrimmage; Walt Sweeney, our defensive end (now an all-pro guard for the San Diego Chargers) also got a couple of good shots at him. Davis was the greatest college runner I ever played against and it was a thrill to do a good job against him, especially since I was only a freshman. After this scrimmage, I knew I was going to make it in college ball.

Along with this excitement, however, came disillusionment. I was soon baptized into the corruption of college athletics. One of the big shocks of my freshman year was finding out that a lot of the guys were getting paid money underneath the table. John Charette, Walt Sweeney, my roommate Jim Gaskins and I were sitting in my room rapping about football, and Charette in his deep nasal voice casually asked, "How much are you guys getting?" I asked, "Getting?" and he said, "Yeah, I'm getting 60 a month." Sweeney acknowledged he was getting a similar amount. Gaskins and I were only receiving the straight N.C.A.A. scholarship—books, tuition and room and board—and we just looked at each other.

Charette further explained the deal: "I'm getting 60 a month and have a free charge account down at Wells & Coverly." Wells & Coverly was the most expensive men's store in Syracuse. Charette was no naive freshman. He had been raised in a small logging town in New Hampshire and had boxed semi-professionally for a few years. His family had been poor, and it was a way to make some money. He told us he wasn't about to take a cut in pay when he came to Syracuse and that was why he had insisted on getting the deal he had.

Eventually, John lost interest in football and didn't show up for practice his junior year. Normally at Syracuse, when a guy refused to go out for practice his scholarship was terminated immediately. But somehow John managed to stay for another two years and collect his money. The rumor among the players was that John had threatened to turn over copies of the Wells and Coverly receipts to N.C.A.A. officials if his scholarship, charge accounts or "spending money" were cut. In our senior year John never practiced. Still, I would occasionally see him coming out of Schwartzwalder's office with his brown manila envelope.

After Charette and Sweeney had left, Gaskins and I sat in our room talking about what we should do. We were angry and upset, not at Sweeney or Charette, but with

Coach Bell who had repeatedly told both Gaskins and myself that the deal at Syracuse covered only room, board, tuition and books. I'd heard about some college players receiving under-the-table payments when I was in high school, but I thought of myself as a pure amateur athlete and I wanted to make sure I went to a college where such practices didn't exist. I had even mentioned this to Coach Bell when he was recruiting me, and he assured me that nothing like this went on at Syracuse. In fact, one of the arguments Bell and the other Syracuse coaches made against my going to LSU was that athletes were paid to go there.

Our first game my freshman year was against Colgate and we beat them 32-0. The game was rather uneventful except that my friend Bill Davidson, playing end for Colgate, knocked out one of my front teeth. I came off the field with my mouth full of blood, and when I pulled out my mouthpiece most of my tooth came with it, leaving the nerve hanging there exposed and smarting. I showed Dick Beyer, the assistant frosh coach, and he told me "It's only your tooth, put your mouthpiece back on. You're the only center we've got." I played the rest of the game and then spent a few hours that evening in the dentist's chair getting the exposed nerve pulled out.

The following week we played the Army Plebes at West Point. We arrived on a beautiful fall day, so the drab greyness of West Point really stood out. The place was like a prison. That night we ate dinner in the huge cadets' dining hall which was filled with row after row of tables, each seating about 12 cadets. A plebe was required to sit at the end of each table, balancing his tail bone right on the edge of his chair, squaring his fork in the air every time he took a bite. But the food never seemed to reach their mouths: every time a plebe started to eat, one of the upperclassmen at the table would scream, "Mr. Schmitz, put down that fork and let's hear a song." The plebe would get up and start singing. No sooner would he sit down and begin eating than another upper classman would holler, "Mr. Schmitz, pour some water." This went on the whole meal.

We were sitting at guest tables right in the middle of these guys and this bullshit blew our minds. We were a pretty sloppy group—though we wore ties as the coaches ordered, we were still hanging out all over. The military atmosphere put us uptight, and the more polite we tried to be the more we fucked up. Guys were accidentally dropping food on the floor and John Mackey knocked over the milk pitcher while lunging for a roll.

Immediately after dinner the cadets held a pep rally in the dining hall. The Army varsity was scheduled to play the Air Force Academy that weekend in New York, so there were a lot of skits and short speeches by retired army officers putting down the Air Force. Each skit or speech was met with mad, fanatical cheering—cadets would scream, stand on their chairs and pound on the tables. We began to get a little intimidated because we thought we would have to face this kind of fanatical behavior on the playing field the next day.

That night I was lying in bed trying to sleep, but every few minutes I'd hear a loud clatter on the cement underneath my window, and it would be some cadet running by at full tilt. I later learned these were plebes who had to double time it everywhere they went when in the barracks area. Between the running plebes and our nervousness about the game most of us couldn't go to sleep. We sat on our bunks rapping about how relaxing it was to be up at Syracuse. Compared to the cadets we felt like professionals, for we had a pretty easy life except on the football field. We got into a long discussion on why anyone would want to go to West Point and agreed unanimously that the cadets must be crazy.

The next afternoon we played the plebes in a cold sleeting rain. The cadets had a lot of spirit and hit pretty hard but, compared to what we were used to up at Syracuse, they were like a good high school team. We tore them up with some of our army veterans really working out on these future officers. We just went out and methodically beat the plebes and left.

We eventually finished with an undefeated freshman season. Meanwhile, the varsity was 7 and 0 and the number one ranked college team in the nation. It was exciting to be a part of the football program at that time, for it seemed all the energies of the university were being channelled toward making sure we won the National Championship. Most of the varsity players had stopped going to classes and were devoting full time to football. Besides the regular afternoon practices, much of each day was spent in special team meetings. The athletic department had complete backing from the administration in this quest for a national championship. Les Dye, the Director of Admissions, had started at Syracuse as a football coach and made sure good players were admitted. Eric Faigle, the Dean of the College of Liberal Arts, was an avid supporter of the football program and the rumor was no professor was about to incur his wrath and rule a player ineligible simply because he wasn't attending classes or taking exams. Even though most of the players hadn't seen a classroom for some time, no one was declared ineligible and the team went on to win the National Championship and defeat Texas in the Cotton Bowl.

Syracuse recruited top football players regardless of their academic ability, and the athletic department's biggest jobs were to get the football players admitted and then to keep them eligible. I remember one citizenship course which all Syracuse freshmen, including football players in the remedial program, were required to take. I knew most of the other players hadn't been to class or done any studying and I couldn't figure out how they were going to pass the exam. Then, just before midterms, we had a squad meeting with one of the tutors hired by the athletic department. The tutor didn't exactly give us the test questions but he did give us a lot of important information. He told us cryptically that if we copied down what he said we would do all right on the exam. He wasn't joking: when I took the exam I discovered he had given us the answers to the test questions. When the general tutoring session broke up, the tutor asked about ten ball players to stay. These were the guys who were really out of it and made no pretense about being students. They had neither the ability nor the interest to do college work. I don't know exactly what kind of help they got after we left, but I do know it was this kind of tutoring that kept them eligible for four years.

There were even less ethical techniques than these.

For example, my brother, Dennis, who also came up to Syracuse on a football scholarship, flunked his freshman year. He was told he would have to get six units of "A" during summer school to get back in school and be eligible for football. After registering for summer school, Dennis immediately drove back to Ohio, where he spent the summer working for a Cleveland construction company. He returned to Syracuse in September with six units of "A" for courses he had never attended.

By the time I graduated, I knew it was next to impossible to be a legitimate student and a football player too. There is a clear conflict, and it is always resolved on the side of the athletic program. Nearly every major university in the country has an employee within the athletic department who supposedly provides athletes with tutorial assistance. At the University of Texas, he is known as the Brain Coach, while at Berkeley he has the more prestigious title of Academic Coordinator. Whatever he is called, his task is always the same: to keep athletes eligible by whatever means necessary, even if it involves getting them an early look at exams, or hiring graduate students to write their term papers or to take finals for them.

Most athletes are accustomed to being on the take and think the system works for them or that they are somehow beating it. But the reality is quite different, and, as in most other things, the athlete is far more sinned against than sinning. He is a commodity and he is treated with unbelievable cynicism. The minute his eligibility expires, the athletic department's concern for his welfare suddenly evaporates. The free tutoring stops and an athlete finds himself faced with a flock of difficult classes which somebody has put off to keep him eligible. He finds himself encased in the stereotype of the dumb jock and psychologically devastated. Of the 26 players who got football scholarships in my freshman year, only John Mackey (now an all-pro end with Baltimore), Gene Stancin and I graduated with our class.

But I didn't know all this until long after my freshman year. At that time I knew only that we had been undefeated and that the varsity was the number one ranked team in the nation.

4

I WAS STILL PLAYING CENTER when spring practice began my freshman year. Jim Ringo, a former Syracuse
player and all-pro center for the Green Bay Packers, had
come back to play in the Varsity-Alumni game, as he did
every year. He came a week early, and spent a lot of time
working with me and the other centers. Jim was the kind
of ball player I wanted to be. He had a very cool kind of
piercing look and was super-dedicated about football. He
had the quality of a killer about him that I really wanted
to master—a rapier-like football player. It was also easy
for me to identify with him because he, too, was light for
his position, weighing only 230 while the average pro center comes in at about 250.

I remember him getting out of his big white Cadillac
when he drove up to the practice field. He had on a dark
green jacket with the white Green Bay Packer patch on it.
After he started working out with us, I would stay with
him until long after the regular practice was over. Jim was
a very patient teacher, and he taught me three major
blocking techniques. The first one was a stab block where

you took a short jab step and stabbed out with your head into the opponent's chin. As he raises up a bit you slam your forearm into his chest, all the time driving furiously with your feet. The second was a reverse crab block where you shot your body toward the defensive guard's inside leg, spinning around so you would be on all fours in front of him. The strategy here was to tie up the defensive guard rather than blow him out of the hole. The third technique was a straight out crab block where you would shoot for his outside leg to cut him off from pursuing the play. Ringo showed me that on all these techniques the important thing was being quick off the ball. It was his incredible quickness that enabled Jim to be an All-Pro center despite his small size.

One afternoon after we got to know each other he showed me one of his special techniques which, he said, would take care of any guy trying to fool around with you. He told me to pretend I was a linebacker. Then he got down into his stance opposite me, shooting off the ball and slamming his hand down on the bridge of my foot. This jammed it into the ground and caught my cleats in the turf. He then drove his shoulder into the outside of my knee. I went down in a heap and when I got up my knee was really hurting. "I only did that about quarter speed," he told me. "If you do it full speed you can fuck up a guy's knee pretty bad." I had learned one of the brutal weapons of an All-Pro player, and I felt really special.

Later that afternoon Jim talked to me about his philosophy of the game. He set the ball down between us and stared at it. "Dave," he said solemnly, "in football, the Commies are on one side of this ball and we're on the other. That's what this game is all about, make no mistake about it." I was really with him. I remember telling him, "Yeah, that's really true." He went on to say that the quick teams win in football just like quick armies win wars.

Later that week we had the final scrimmage before the alumni game. I was practicing what Jim taught me and getting off the ball very quickly. The quarterback called a 33 quick trap and my assignment was to block the defensive guard. I shot off the ball so quickly I missed the snap to the quarterback but I got a tremendous block on the defensive guard; I took him down the line of scrimmage and opened a wide hole. Then a teammate fell on my outstretched ankle and really tore it up. I was lying on the ground rolling in pain and heard Ben Schwartzwalder say to Ringo, "Damn, that Meggyesy made a hell of a block, too bad he blew the snap." Ben then moved the players a short distance away and continued the scrimmage.

The injury I received meant I couldn't play in the alumni game that weekend. At first they thought my ankle was broken, though it turned out to be a bad sprain, and I was on crutches for a few weeks. But the only thing I could think of was that I wouldn't be able to play against Ringo.

I went through a process of degeneration once I realized I couldn't play. I began boozing it pretty heavily, going out and getting drunk just about every night. I remember one night when I came back from the Clover Club. I was standing on my crutches in the quadrangle in front of my dorm, screaming at the top of my lungs, "Fuck the Resident Advisor [Resident Advisors—RAs—

were grad students assigned to watch over the floors. Some were all right; others acted like cops.] You son of a bitch, come out here, you motherfucker." I was waving my crutches like a madman. Jim Gaskins, my roommate, came out and helped me stagger up the stairs. I stopped at the RA's door and began pounding on it. I then opened a quart of beer I had with me and poured it under his door. All this time I was still screaming for the RA to get his ass out in the hall. When the RA opened the door he told me to get to bed or he'd call the police. He was scared, but I could tell that he was asking himself what else could he expect from a dumb jock.

Every time I or the other freshmen ballplayers got frustrated we would engage in the sort of behavior everybody expected of jocks—animals who were at best half-domesticated. We usually took it out on the RAs. Once we got the key to an RA's room, filled his wastebasket full of paper and set it in the middle of the room. We kept watch at his window and when Jim, my roommate, spotted him strolling back across the quad, we lit the basket on fire and ran out of the room closing the door behind us. We hid in the bathroom so we could see him coming down the hall. By this time the burning smell had spread throughout the floor and some smoke was beginning to seep out from under his door. He saw the smoke and began screaming, "My room is on fire, my room is on fire, ring the fire alarm." On his orders we willingly tripped the alarm. Bells started ringing throughout the dorm. He opened the door to his room and was engulfed in smoke. The smoke quickly died down and he saw the smoldering waste basket. He ran to the bathroom to get some water to douse the fire. Putting the wastebasket out in the hall he began yelling, "Goddamn football players."

The coaches saw this as sowing wild oats. Ben viewed Gaskins and myself as two of his "good boys" because of our aggressive hustle. For this reason we were regularly asked to take care of the high school recruits when they came around for the weekend. The high school players would usually arrive in Syracuse on Friday afternoon and stay until Sunday morning, and Jim and I would be responsible for setting them up in a hotel, feeding and entertaining them for the weekend. I got approximately 50 dollars for expenses to take care of each recruit, and immediately pocketed at least 25 of that, then spent the rest of the weekend trying to take care of them as cheaply as possible. Friday night we would sneak them into the college dining hall and feed them free, really stuffing them up. After dinner, Jim and I would take them to a campus movie where, by borrowing a few ID cards, we could get them in free. When the movie let out we walked down to the Clover Club. Irving, the bartender, was an avid follower of the Syracuse football team and would supply us with pitchers of beer for half price. These high school guys would really get drunk fast. They were supposed to be put up in hotels but we'd get them drunk enough so they wouldn't mind sleeping on the floor in our dormitory room. They'd stagger in, take a couple of blankets and then pass out on the floor, waking up the next morning really hung over. Saturday it was roughly the same procedure except we would take them to a fraternity party where the beer was free.

In a few weeks my ankle improved so I was able to

walk without crutches and I gradually got myself back together. I finished my freshman year at Syracuse with moderate success academically and went home to Solon eagerly awaiting the upcoming football season. There was a lot of talk about repeating as National Champions and I wanted to make sure I was part of the team.

5

As soon as I got back to Solon I went out looking for a construction job. My rap was, "I'm a football player from Syracuse University. I'm looking for a job to build me up over the summer and I'll work very hard for you if you'll give me a chance." I wasn't having any luck, and Mr. Davidson told me you should always get dressed up when looking for a job—wear a suit and tie, shine your shoes, have your hair trimmed and nails clipped. That didn't seem to make much sense with the sort of work I was looking for, but I followed his suggestion and went to a big construction site near Akron. It was all muddy and I stood there in my Ivy League suit looking like Lord Fauntleroy at a street fight. I went to the superintendent's shack and went through my spiel. "I think the concrete people need a man, go over and talk to Izzy," he said, and I went to look for this Izzy. Some workers told me he was up on the roof where they were pouring a big air conditioning pad. I climbed up on the roof and yelled to him over the noise of the machinery, "Izzy. I'm looking for a job." He turned to look me over and swung the vibrator he was operating so that it threw a bunch of concrete on my pants. He slowly looked me over and said "O.K."

The construction superintendent would come out every now and then during that summer and say, "Hey Meggyesy, this isn't like playing football, is it?" It sure as hell wasn't. We were pouring 20-foot wide sections of the warehouse floor and we were usually standing in concrete over our ankles. It was really back-breaking work most of the time, and we were always doubled over smoothing out the concrete in the bays.

I was on the job for about ten days when the superintendent came out and told me, "Meggyesy get a shovel." I knew what he was up to. A truck was waiting to dump a full load of concrete, and my job was to get behind the truck and level off the concrete as it came out of the truck. We were filling a bay ten feet wide and the test was if I could work fast enough so the truck wouldn't need to stop. This was my big macho test. I got in behind the truck with my shovel and emptied the full load of concrete without stopping. I met the test, and after that they stopped referring sarcastically to me as "the college football player."

Later that summer I had my first experience with unions. I was working as well as or better than any of the guys on the construction crew. One day we were pouring a bay that was a little deeper than normal, so the work was much harder, and I was pouring sweat. The union business agent drove up in a big white Imperial, and got out wearing a silk suit and alligator shoes. He didn't say a word to me. He just put a card between two of his fingers and flipped it into my face. I was ready to smash him in the head with my shovel when Izzy stepped between us. The business agent told me to be down at his office in Akron at eight that night and walked away. I had no intention of going to see this guy, but Izzy told me he had threatened to shut down the job if I didn't join the union, so even though I was really pissed off I drove into Akron that night and joined up.

I went to a few union meetings and watched how the leaders handled union funds. Three of them would sit up in front and mumble and mumble. Eventually they'd say something like "There's a motion on the floor that $5,000 be designated to Saint Vincent's Home for Boys. Any discussion?" And there would be none. "All opposed." None. "All in favor, OK it's passed." It was clear to me they were lining somebody's pockets. I've never been opposed to unions, but ever since that summer I've been opposed to most union leaders.

Looking back, I remember that summer as a time of order and security. I was making good money, $3.89 an hour, and getting in shape for football. My girl friend at Syracuse, Stacy, who is now my wife, came down to see me a couple of times. There were no hassles. It was kind of a glorious dead summer. I wasn't thinking about anything too much, and there was little ambiguity in my life.

Football practice began at Syracuse on September 1st, and I wanted to be in top shape so after work I began working out about two hours every evening starting in mid-July with Bill Davidson. We'd loosen up by throwing the football around for about 20 minutes, do calisthenics for 30 minutes, and then spend about an hour running a combination of distance and sprints.

Bill did a lot of weight-lifting that summer, which

didn't interest me. One evening, Bill was doing bench presses and bet me I couldn't bench 300 pounds, the maximum amount he had to put on the bar. I plunked down on the bench and quickly snapped up the 300 pounds, even though I only weighed about 205.

I reported for pre-season drills in the greatest shape of my life with the express purpose of trying at least to make the traveling squad. Even though we had lost a lot of guys through graduation everybody expected that with the return of Ernie Davis and the nucleus of the 1959 team we would still be able to repeat as National Champions. I had a reputation from spring ball as one of Ben's hustling "good boys" and I was always a little segregated from the rest of the players. One incident during pre-season drills vividly brought this separation home to me: one evening after practice some guys were playing cards and a few of us were standing around the table urging them on. It was the first time I had been with a group of varsity players informally and I was nervous being there. I repeated some phrase of encouragement that I'd heard one of the other guys use. I used the right words, but I said them a shade too loud. Everybody stopped. The guy who was holding the cards turned around and glared at me. It was like he said, "Listen you hustling son of a bitch, you're not wanted here."

But despite the reputation I was getting I continued to be a real fanatic on the football field. I never walked anywhere, in fact I never even jogged: once on the field, I sprinted everywhere I went. Also, I had this thing about being first in line at any drills. My first few days at fall practice I was the first sophomore in line for each drill.

Once I learned the different drills I sprinted to be first in line. I'd have sacrificed my life for the team and I think the coaches knew it.

One day we had one of Ben's little extra exercises. We always ran laps at the end of practice, but this day he decided to have all the teams on the squad run a relay race against each other. Each guy had to run a quarter mile. At that time I was playing tackle on the fourth team. I was the anchor man, and we were in last place when I started out. Just before I got the baton, Rock Pirro, the offensive line coach, turned to Ted Daily,who coached defense, and said "I'll bet you five that Meggyesy takes it." I heard them talking and I was excited—even though I was on the fourth string they knew who I was. I took off with the baton like a shot, passed everybody and came in first. Our prize for winning the race was an extra bottle of Pepsi after practice. It was always hot and humid in Syracuse during pre-season drills in early September, and we were not allowed to drink anything on the practice field. Consequently, nothing ever tasted better than the bottle of iced Pepsi we received after each practice. The first thing each player would do when he hit the locker room was to get his cold Pepsi from the equipment manager. You could learn a lot about each ball player by watching how he drank his bottle. Some of them would knock it off in one gulp as soon as they got it. There were also guys who would go through a whole self control ritual, putting the bottle in their lockers and not drinking it until after they had taken off all their equipment.

One particular incident during pre-season drills my sophomore year was, I suppose, the turning point in my football career, the outcome of which had the chance of making or breaking me as a football player. For me playing always meant walking a fragile line between being an all out hitter and just simply saying I'm going to hang it up. I started pre-season drills on the fifth team, but in a couple of days I was moved to fourth team. We were having a scrimmage against the second team and I was playing defensive tackle across from George Frankovitch, a 245-pound tackle. Something happened to me and I just didn't want to hit. I couldn't say anything to the coaches so I kept on playing but I kept ducking my head and Frankovitch was really putting it to me. Coach Daily, the defensive line coach, stopped the scrimmage and screamed at me, "Meggyesy, God damn you, you can't duck your head in this game. Get the hell out of here." I almost started crying right there as I walked off the field. All the other guys were looking at me and wondering what the hell I was going to do. I had been ducking my head because I was scared and I knew it. I just didn't want to hit; I didn't want to go against this guy.

Two days later, on Saturday, I was scheduled opposite Frankovitch again. This was the first really big scrimmage of the year, and it was going to be filmed. I'd done a lot of thinking over the two days since the last scrimmage and I was super psyched right from the start. I really began to put it to Frankovitch. It got so bad that after the tenth play Ben came out and began screaming at him, "You kicked the shit out of him Thursday, why can't you touch him today." I was making tackles in the backfield, just eating his lunch, really murdering him.

When we took a break in the scrimmage, Ben walked over toward me, took an orange jersey off the back of one

of the third string lineman—at Syracuse they used different colored jersies to distinguish the pecking order—and
told me to put it on. This was the only time Schwartzwalder actually made a promotion on the practice field
during my four years at Syracuse. Now that I was on the
third team, I was on the traveling squad and there was a
good chance that I might even be playing.

During scrimmages at Syracuse, the first team went
against the third and the second went against the fourth.
So when the scrimmage resumed after the break I was
going against the first team. I continued having a tremendous day—I even caught the two first string halfbacks,
Ernie Davis and Mark Weber, a couple of times in the
backfield. On one particular play, Davis had come up to
the line just as I fought off a block. He saw me slide into
the hole and began moving laterally down the line. I
sprinted after him and caught him from behind.

I did get a bruised shoulder that day, and spent Monday morning in the training room getting it treated. The
rest of the team, except for the few of us who were injured, was at a squad meeting in the gym. Neal Pratt, one
of the trainers, came to where I was sitting with a hot pack
on my shoulder and told me, "Wow, Ben's really saying
some really nice things about you in the meeting." After I
finished my treatment, I drove up to the gym with some of
the other injured ball players, because everyone had to be
at the meeting when the film started. We arrived just as
the film was about to begin. Ben stopped what he was
saying and turned to me, "Meggyesy, Saturday you had
the finest scrimmage I've ever seen anyone play in my 12
years up here at Syracuse. We really have high hopes for

you." Then he turned to the rest of the squad and said, "I want you people to pay particular attention to this guy in the film. This is the kind of desire and dedication we want around here. If you younger guys want to play ball for us, play like this guy."

I was excited but felt ambivalent about Ben's remarks. On one hand I was tremendously happy over the praise and approval. But on the other hand, those few words defined me, more clearly than before, as apart from the rest of the guys on the team. Ben had singled me out emphatically as one of the good boys, and I could feel the animosity of the veteran players. The team even gave me a nickname: "Super Psych." It wasn't hard to see why. I remember standing and bullshitting with another player one day (something I rarely did because I was always very intent about practice) so that I didn't hear Schwartzwalder when he called the first team together to run some plays. They were lined up and ready to go with an empty space at right tackle. Schwartzwalder hollered at me, "Meggyesy get in here." I was only about ten yards away, but instead of jogging up to the line and taking my place, I sprinted over and immediately dropped into my stance. I could hear snickering from the players standing in the background. Later that afternoon I overheard one of the wealthy alums who used to come out and watch practice saying, "That Meggyesy kid is a coach's dream."

At Syracuse there's a tradition about the pre-game meal. We would always go out to a country club a few miles from the university about 9:00, and eat a breakfast of orange juice, steak, scrambled eggs, tea and toast. Nutritionally, it's been demonstrated time and again that a

pre-game meal should consist of foods high in carbohy-
drates, but most football coaches insist on a high protein
meal capped off with a semi-raw steak. I guess they think
that tearing into a piece of bloody meat gets a player in
the right frame of mind for hitting.

There was great prestige, but also great pressure involved in having been the number one team in the country
the previous year. The 1959 National Champion squad
had started an unbeaten streak, and now we faced a situation where every victory extended our winning streak and
preserved our number one ranking.

The first game that year was against Boston University. I didn't expect to play too much because I was still on
the third team, playing behind Lou Mautino and John
Brown (who went on to play with the Cleveland Browns
and is now with the Pittsburgh Steelers.) I was so excited
that as soon as we returned to the dorm from our pre-
game meal I immediately threw up my raw steak. Though
I lay on my bed trying to calm myself, I was totally frantic. I was thinking about all the things I was going to do to
Boston University, the kind of mayhem I was going to
wreak on them. I finally got to play during the last quarter
of the game. On my first play, the Boston quarterback was
tackled for about a ten yard loss. I didn't get first shot at him
and came in on the pile a half second too late. The referee
went for his flag and almost threw it. He yelled at me,
"Number 57, do that again and it's going to cost you 15."
After that first hit I was okay, and calmed down. I played
defense most of the last quarter. I got the quarterback twice
while he was trying to pass and made some other good
plays. It was my first varsity game and I felt really good

about my performance even though I had only played briefly.

Stacy had come in from Rochester for the game and we went to a post game fraternity party. The Syracuse fraternities rushed the jocks hard. Each house wanted its "house jock," to use for attracting pledges. When I entered that fraternity house, the people there all acted as if they knew me even though I had never met most of them. One of the members took me around introducing me to people, saying, "This is Dave Meggyesy. Dave's a sophomore football player here, the guy who made those spectacular defensive plays this afternoon." He told me all of his brothers were proud of the way I played and that he hoped I would become a Phi Delt. That invitation and the party were part of the payoff for being a football player at Syracuse; the adulation accorded the college football hero. Although I was very pleased about it at the time, I felt out of place there and never joined.

During my sophomore year, I would conceptualize myself as a particular kind of ball player, and play accordingly. I felt that if I thought of myself as a big, rough son of a bitch I would brutalize my opponent. On the other hand, if I thought of myself as a lean, slashing, quick-hitting guy, I'd play a different way. After the Boston game, when I was out-weighed by 35 pounds, I decided to concentrate on the latter style. It fit in with my purist approach to football—I never wore hand pads or taped my hands up in any way, and I even cut off my jersey above the elbows and refused to wear elbow pads. For me, getting psyched up for a game meant building a mental image of this rapier-like ball player who would slash them wide open.

The second game of the season was against Kansas, one of the top-ranked teams in the country. They had three outstanding backs, John Hadl (now of the San Diego Chargers) at quarterback, and Bert Coan and Curtiss McClinton at the halfbacks. Coan and McClinton had 9.6 speed and Hadl was as fast as anyone we had on our team. Roy Simmons, our defensive backfield coach, had scouted them during their opening game and summed up his impressions by warning us, "Boys, they're lean, mean and racy." Kansas' favorite play was a quarterback option, where their linemen would get down into a four point stance and try to scramble-block you. They were small, light and really quick and they didn't try to overpower you; they would try to tie you up with this scramble blocking. On the option play Hadl would take the snap, pivot, fake into the line with his fullback and then slide down into the line with the ball. McClinton would trail behind him so Hadl had the option of either carrying the ball himself off tackle or flipping it out to McClinton for a sweep. Whenever I saw this play coming I would blast across the line and meet Hadl in his own backfield—it got so I'd be flying in there and completely blowing up the play before it got started. We ran all over Kansas, gaining more than 300 yards on the ground to their 68, but we just snuck by with a 14-7 victory to continue our unbeaten streak for another week. I played half the game and played well. Afterwards I heard Ben tell the reporters that I was the finest defensive lineman the team had.

Our next game was against Holy Cross at Worcester,

Massachusetts. They were never a major power, and Ben kept them on the schedule each year as a breather. We couldn't get up for the game and they almost beat us. When we were leaving the field after the game, the Holy Cross fans were chanting "You ain't number one no more." And sure enough, when the rankings came out the following week, we weren't number one any more even though we had continued our unbeaten streak through fourteen games. But while the team as a whole played poorly, I had the most spectacular game of my college career up to that point. We were behind 6-0 at half time and Ben was furious at most of the players—but he singled me out for praise. "There's only one person in here who's playing football and that's Meggyesy," he told us. "The rest of you guys are candy asses, you're not fit to be national champions." He really chewed them out. His praise made me feel good but it was one more step in alienating me from the rest of the team because the guys were pissed at me for constantly being paraded before them as the model football player.

I received my first under-the-table payment after this game. Bob Stem, our starting center, walked out of the locker room with me after the game. Stem was a big square-headed cat from New Jersey, a real rough, hard-drinking, hard-fighting kind of a guy. He had played a good game against Holy Cross, too, and we were walking together toward the team bus when Rock Pirro, offensive line coach, came up to see us. Rock took hold of my hand and I didn't know what he wanted so I started shaking hands with him. He said, "Nice game." I thanked him and began to walk away when I realized he had put a $20 bill in my hand. He saw the startled look on my face and told me, "It's all right Dave, an alum asked me to give it to you." He then did the same thing with Stem. I felt funny about taking it, but I just put the money in my pocket and didn't say anything.

The previous year, it had been common knowledge among the players that the stars were picking up anywhere from $20 to $50 after each game. More players were involved in the latter half of the season when Syracuse was climbing in the polls and closing in on the number one ranking. In my experience, the coaches usually gave out the money in a handshake like Rock Pirro had, but often they just handed the players a brown envelope with the money enclosed. Sometimes they varied it: on one occasion, after a home game, I was trying to get my street shoe on and couldn't figure out what was causing the discomfort. I tipped it up and a crumpled $20 bill fell out of the toe.

In the fourth game my sophomore year we met our arch-rivals Penn State. Our win streak was now at 14 games and after our poor showing against Holy Cross many people expected Penn State to beat us. Over 40,000 people packed into Archibald Stadium on a blazing hot afternoon—the largest home game crowd in the history of Syracuse University football. After my performance against Holy Cross, I started this game.

We were leading 21-15 up to the last few minutes of the game. Then Penn State went 84 yards down the field to our two yard line. A touchdown would give them a tie, and if they made the conversion it would break our win streak. I was in on defense for the entire drive and the heat—it was humid and about 85°—had really gotten to me. Between plays I would wait on all fours trying to get my breath back. The ball was on our two-yard line, and I was down in my stance waiting for the next play. I was really groggy and thinking "OK, you bastards, one more play and time's going to run out." I looked at the clock and saw there were seven seconds left in the game. In trying to get myself psyched up, I completely lost touch, even forgot what down it was. The Penn State players were lined up across from me, but when I looked around I realized I was the only Syracuse player on the line. My teammates were huddling behind me, for we had stopped Penn State on the previous play. I got up and some of the guys yelled at me to get in the huddle. We called a quarterback sneak and time ran out. We had won our fifteenth straight game, 21-15.

The fifth game of the season was against West Virginia down in Morgantown. Besides starting defensive tackle, I was now also starting as offensive tackle. The team was really together after our victory over Penn State and we had our best game of the year against West Virginia, beating them 45-0. Ernie Davis and Art Baker each scored two touchdowns, and John Mackey and Walt Sweeney each scored on pass reception. West Virginia didn't score, but they got in some extracurricular hits. I remember the first time I threw a downfield block, their defensive back just stood there. I was thinking, "Christ, this guy isn't even trying to defend himself." Then as I started to launch my body he cranked up and punched me in the mouth. It was a left hook. By the fourth quarter the game had evolved into a street brawl.

The plane back to Syracuse left from the Pittsburgh

Airport (a two hour bus ride from Morgantown). A lot of the guys were boozing it up pretty good with pints of liquor they'd sneaked on board. Mark Weber and I were sitting together during the bus ride and he was telling me how worried he was about the team getting overconfident, especially since we had beaten West Virginia so badly. He was concerned because some of the veterans on the team no longer seemed willing to put out. They took another National Championship for granted, and they were getting involved in too many other things besides football. I agreed with Mark because I too was bothered by the attitude of some of the veteran ball players.

Our next game was against Pittsburgh, the last formidable team we had to play. Foreseeing the dramatic possibilities of this game, the more entrepreneurial-minded veterans had bought blocks of tickets before the season to scalp before our two big home games against Pitt and Penn State. One of these guys was our end, Fred Mautino. We were driving back to the dorm from the pre-game breakfast when we passed the stadium and Fred shouted at the bus driver to stop. Everyone wondered what the hell he was doing, because most of us were busy getting psyched up for the game. There were no coaches present and the bus driver let Fred off. We saw him pull out this enormous wad of tickets and begin to sell them to the early arrivals for the game. When the rest of us got back to rest in our rooms before going to get dressed, I lay down on my bed thinking about Fred and his goddamn tickets and got pissed off at him for his lack of interest in the game.

About an hour later, I walked over to the locker room to get dressed. I always dressed in a certain way. I put my pants on first, my socks and shoes next, and then I'd go through the ritual of tying my shoes correctly. If my shoes were tied too tight or too loose I felt I couldn't play. Then I'd put on my shoulder pads and jersey, test the snaps on my helmet, check the screws on my face mask and then put my helmet on. I went through the whole ritual that day, but I was so psyched for this game it took me about 12 tries to get my shoelaces correct.

The game began and Pitt was ready. So was their end, Mike Ditka, who was Mautino's rival that year for All American honors. Fred had been an All American the year before as a junior when he played on the National Championship team, but many people felt Ditka was a better end. The word was out that only one of them would be selected from the East on the 1960 All-American teams—this was standard procedure since the selectors wanted national geographic distribution on the teams. So the game was not only a contest between two particularly rugged football squads, but also a showdown between two rugged guys.

I played next to Fred on offense and defense, so I was in a good position to see Ditka tear him up. Pitt used their famous State 7 defense where Ditka and the other end would come crashing down the line. Fred would be blown over. Just as I'd start to block on my own man, I'd hear the referee's whistle signaling the play was over. I'd look behind me and see this pile of bodies where Ditka had driven Fred into the blocking back and the ball carrier, completely destroying the play. This went on for most of the afternoon, and by the fourth quarter, Ditka was blowing into our backfield almost at will.

Ditka was just as effective against Fred when Pitt had the ball. I remember one particular play that Pitt had great success with all afternoon. It was an option play where the quarterback either handed the ball off to the fullback into an off-tackle hole, pitched it out to his halfback or kept it himself. One time when they used this play, the fullback made a great fake into the line. I went for it and really blasted him. I hit him a sharp heavy blow and we both went down. I looked up and beside me Ditka had Mautino laying on his back as the quarterback kept the ball and ran through Fred's hole for a touchdown. Ditka's conquest of Mautino was a microcosm of the way the game went that afternoon. Pitt shut us out 10-0 ending our undefeated streak at 16 games. We were badly beaten and we all felt it. Pitt had out-hit and out-hustled us all afternoon and their victory was no fluke.

We also lost our next game against Army, 9-6, in New York City. I got a big thrill out of playing in the home of the New York Yankees, but I'll always remember that game for something else. Mark Weber had suffered a succession of knee injuries during the season, and there was some question about whether he would be able to play against Army. Mark was seriously thinking about quitting football. About a month earlier, he had asked Ben to cut him in on some of the money other players were getting. Ben flatly refused. Mark and I talked about it a lot, and he decided to stick it out because it was his last year.

He didn't even finish that year. In the second half of the Army game, Ben sent Mark in to receive a punt—something he was almost never called on to do. Mark caught it and started up field. One of Army's big tackles got a clean shot on his bad knee and just tore it up. Mark was carried off the field on a stretcher. It just didn't make sense to have a big, heavy guy with a bad knee returning a punt which everyone knows is one of the most hazardous plays in the game. Mark never played football again.

The last game of the year we flew down to Florida to play the University of Miami in the Orange Bowl. This was the first time I received a serious injury. Late in the second half the Miami quarterback handed off to his halfback on a quick hitter over my hole. I got a clean shot at him at the line of scrimmage and belted him fairly hard. I was driving him to the ground when John Saketa, one of our defensive guards, piled into my knee. My spikes had caught in the ground so my knee and ankle took the full impact of his blow. They carried me off. My knee was sticking out and looked badly damaged. Doc Barney, our team physician, gave my leg a whack just below the knee and popped it back into place. Two trainers then carried me into the locker room on a stretcher. The pain was excruciating for I had also torn up my ankle and it was hemorrhaging. The trainers put me on a table, told me an ambulance was on its way, then went back out to watch the game. It was eerie to hear the fans screaming as I lay alone in the locker room not knowing how badly I was hurt. I felt completely cut off, and I was scared that it might be the end of my career.

The ambulance finally arrived and I was taken to the hospital still wearing most of my equipment. They took x-rays and the nurses packed my knee and ankle with ice.

Then the hospital also seemed to forget about me; I was just lying in the emergency room waiting for something to happen. A nurse who was going off duty came in and we began talking. She introduced herself—Beverly was her name—and asked if she could get me anything. I said, "Yeah, I'd love a six pack of beer, it might kill the pain." She left to get some, but before she got back the hospital staff had transferred me upstairs to a private room. I was afraid she wouldn't be able to find me, but as soon as the other nurses left, she came into the room with the beer hidden under her coat. I'd had nothing to eat or drink except a little water since the pre-game meal, so after the first few beers I was smashed. After a while the head nurse came in and told my new friend she had to leave.

The next morning I felt quite a bit better. Jim Decker, Syracuse's assistant athletic director who was traveling with the team, called and told me two alums would be over to take me back to the hotel where the team was staying. I assured him I had a ride—Beverly and I had made plans the previous night to spend the day at the beach. Despite my assurances, Decker insisted on sending someone to pick me up. Just as we were leaving the hospital, these two middle-aged guys started yelling at us. "Meggyesy, Meggyesy wait a minute; we're here to give you a ride back to the hotel." They were leering at Beverly, and I could see they had sized up the situation. They gave me a hard time and kept insisting I had to leave with them. "I'm sorry you guys came out here for me," I told them, "but I told Mr. Decker I had a ride when he called earlier this morning." As we were walking away, I heard them mumbling something about how the coaches weren't going to be happy. The coaches never said anything to me directly, but on the flight back to Syracuse the next morning, they kept looking at me and nodding with a knowing smile.

When the season was over, Ben had a lot of praise for me. He told reporters I was the best interior lineman they had and the best sophomore on the team, even though there were other players on the team like Walt Sweeney and John Mackey who were also sophomores. I was awarded honorable mention All-American honors by the Associated Press.

I was one of Ben's good boys, but I couldn't forget seeing Mark's career end so suddenly and senselessly. The way he was injured made me acutely aware of the incredible brutality of the game and of the power those who control the game have over the players. I also felt I had proven myself as a football player and began to get more interested in other things. While I continued to be the hustling, super-aggressive ball player for the rest of college and my seven years in the NFL, I never again played with the intensity and blind commitment that I had my sophomore year.

6

SCHWARTZWALDER AND I appeared together on a couple of radio and television shows shortly after my sophomore season ended. Since I had won honorable mention All-American honors he was touting me as the next Roger Davis—Syracuse's great All-American lineman who also came from Solon High. I took the praise but, especially after what had happened to Mark Weber, I wasn't playing football for any great love of the game but primarily to win approval. I still felt ambivalent about hitting. At times I didn't want to touch anyone or to be touched. On other occasions I felt great pleasure and release from the sheer physical violence of the game. Sometimes after getting a clean shot at the ball carrier, I would feel this tremendous energy flow and not experience the pain of contact at all. I sometimes could psych myself so high I would feel indestructible. Like most of the other players, I had been introduced to a system of rewards—psychological and material—and I played mainly for them. The intrinsic joy of physicality got shunted into the background. Even now, after playing for 14 years, I can't really say if there is any basic worth to the game. I just can't separate the game from the payoffs—approval, money, adulation.

The process of questioning, which eventually made me decide to get out of football, really began after my successful sophomore season. I had performed well and gotten recognition, but there was no real satisfaction. Shortly after the season ended, I began making friends with graduate students and people in the School of Fine Arts. When Schwartzwalder found out about this he called me into his office. "Dave, you have a great football career ahead of you," he began. "But if you hang around with those beatniks you're going to destroy yourself." I told him they were my friends. "That may be true, Dave, but it doesn't look good for our football team for you to be hanging out with those beatniks." I assured him I would do nothing to hurt the team and left his office.

My beatnik friends, as Ben called them, hung out at a bar near campus called the Orange. Their view of the world and of life was completely different from the football ethic. At first I couldn't believe them. They were completely sacrilegious when it came to athletics. They would get drunk and go to the games to laugh at the fans and mock the coach.

Some of them were drama students and they would do great imitations of Ben, who they called "the pygmy paratrooper" because of his diminutive size and widely publicized war exploits. They would point out the cynicism and hypocrisy of the university's commitment to football: at the same time Chancellor Tolley was claiming to be guided by the highest religious and educational principles, he was hiring football players to gather prestige and money for the university. What my new friends were saying didn't make too much sense to me yet, but I enjoyed rapping with them. My association with these "beatniks" eventually became such a contradiction that I had to stop seeing them whenever I was playing. In the fall and during spring practice I would rarely stop in at the Orange for I knew hanging around there would screw me up for football. I was becoming a man in the middle—unable to commit myself fully to football, but also unable to find any substitute for it.

During the previous year, I had met Stacy Kennedy, now my wife, on a blind date. She was also a freshman, had grown up in nearby Rochester, and was attending the School of Fine Arts at Syracuse. I still remember our first evening together: we sat at a college hangout talking about our hopes and our lives. We cut through the usual man-woman games very quickly, and Stacy soon established herself as the dominant person in my "other life"— the life not related to football. She has continued to play this role, almost since our first meeting, and she saw more clearly and much sooner than I did the dehumanizing impact the game has on the people who play it.

In my sophomore year at Syracuse, Stacy and I continued seeing each other even though she had dropped out of school and was living with her mother in Rochester. When she moved back to Syracuse after Christmas vacation, we began living together, although I was supposed to be living in the football dorm, Sadler Hall. Gene Stancin, my roommate and one of my few friends on the team, tried to cover for me when the coaches and Mr. Davidson became suspicious. Every time they called Gene would tell them I was in the library studying. They began calling later and later until one morning Coach Bell called at 3 a.m. and told Gene he wanted to talk to me. Realizing the library story wouldn't work, Gene told Bell he hadn't seen me since he had come by our apartment for dinner a few weeks before.

Coaches and football players generally have a peculiar attitude towards male-female relationships. At Syracuse the prevailing opinion was that it was somehow healthy and manly to go out and get drunk, pick up some girl, lay her and maybe even rough her up a bit. To the coaches, this was "normal" behavior; but they got upset if you began to develop a genuine relationship with a woman. This was "immoral," and the coaches and many of the players thought Stacy was sinful and I was misguided.

The situation got so bad at one point that a player who had a reputation as a wild man with chicks told Stacy he would kill her if she didn't stop seeing me. And my "good friend" Mark Weber tried to have a long talk with me one afternoon about Stacy's morals. He actually asked, "What kind of girl is she if she's letting you live with her before you're married?" and indicated that the coaching staff was upset over my relationship with Stacy. Once I fully understood what he was getting at, I told Mark never to bother me again with that kind of talk.

Stacy and I got engaged early in the spring and planned to marry in July. In today's atmosphere we probably just would have continued as we were, but that was

1961, and we were getting a little anxious about living together unmarried.

When I drove home at the end of my sophomore year to pick up some clothes, I found out that Bill Davidson was planning to spend the summer driving around the country in one of his parents' cars. One night at dinner Mr. Davidson—who was also against my marrying Stacy—asked me if I would like to go along. I told him I couldn't go even if I wanted to because I didn't have any money. He said he thought the trip would be good for me and offered me $500 to pay for my share of the expenses.

I was excited about the chance to travel around the country with Bill. I was also tired out by all the people arguing against the marriage, so I decided to take Mr. Davidson's offer. When I drove back to Syracuse and told Stacy, she was upset and we postponed the wedding indefinitely. By the time Bill and I left on the trip a couple of days later, I was very unhappy because I felt I had allowed myself to be bought off. The more I thought about it the worse I felt, and the trip seemed to drag on and on. Bill and I returned during the first week in August, and Stacy and I were married in Syracuse on August 19th, two weeks before pre-season practice began.

Though I felt equally able to play on offense or defense, the coaches had typed me as a great defensive player. I had this charge on defense where I'd get down in a four-point stance up on my fingertips—I was constantly squeezing a rubber ball so I could support much of my weight on my fingertips. I was very quick and could usually strike out from this four-point stance and hit the offensive lineman before he was halfway out of his stance.

My style fit in with the theory of playing defense at Syracuse, which was that you had a patch of ground to defend. It was like the domino theory: you kicked the shit out of the guy across from you and if the play was in your area, you got past him and made the tackle or hustled to the ball. Schwartzwalder's philosophy of football precluded any sophisticated defensive techniques such as stunting or threading of keys. He didn't believe in any of the "fancy stuff" as he called it; he simply wanted us to defeat our opponent physically and get the ball carrier.

My quickness compensated for my small size on defense, but I had a much more difficult job trying to block 250 pound defensive tackles when we were on offense. I'd learned from Jim Ringo to be extremely quick off the ball. I knew it was crucial to get "inside" the defensive lineman; once "underneath" him, I could drive him out of the play or shield him from pursuing the ball carrier. I developed a special technique for pass blocking. I'd fire off the ball and stick my opponent under the chin, straightening him up and neutralizing his initial charge. Then I'd let him start to go around me. I could see the gleam in his eyes as he accelerated, thinking he had me beat. I'd trail along beside him while he was penetrating about two or three yards into the backfield, and just as he got close to the quarterback I'd spear him in the legs just above the knees with my helmet. As we went down together I'd keep scrambling to get on top. It was impossible for me to block a 250 pound tackle head on but this technique allowed me to utilize speed and quickness. The only problem with spear blocking was that I got kicked in the head a lot. Every time I drove my head into the defensive tackle's legs, his knee would come driving into my helmet. I'd be pretty dingy by the end of the game and by my senior year I was throwing up after every game.

The most difficult task I had in college football was blocking on running plays: just about every defensive tackle I played against during my career at Syracuse outweighed me by 30 to 40 pounds. There wasn't any one standard technique I could use against these big tackles so I would have to improvise every game.

In the Pitt game my junior year, for instance, I was going against a big 245 pound tackle named Adamcheck. On the first play of the game our quarterback, Dave Sarette, called a quick hitter with Ernie Davis going over my hole. I blasted straight out in an attempt to block Adamcheck, but he caught me under the chin with his forearm, lifted me in the air and knocked me on my ass. He caught Davis just as he was getting the handoff from Sarette. Ernie hadn't gained momentum yet and Adamcheck really blasted him and threw him for a two yard loss. In the huddle Ernie just glared at me and Sarette asked, "What the hell happened with that block?" I mumbled, "I'll get that son of a bitch on the next play," but I was worried because my head was still ringing from Adamcheck's forearm. I'd never been hit that hard on a straight out blocking play and I feared I was in for a long afternoon. I wanted to block him, but I also wanted to avoid his forearm, and I couldn't see any way of doing both. When Sarette called the same play again, I readied myself for Adamcheck's forearm. It was a muddy day and when I went to drive out on the snap of the ball I slipped and almost went down on one knee. But Adamcheck still threw his forearm. I saw it whiz by, missing my face by a few inches. Adamcheck's body was now exposed, and I drove up, stabbing him in the chin with my helmet, and easily moved him out of the hole.

This made me realize that he threw his forearm automatically on the snap of the ball, and if I delayed my charge by half a count I could control him easily. Adamcheck got more and more pissed off as the game wore on. A couple of times when I got him down he tried to kick me in the head. He was cursing furiously, "Meggyesy, you son of a bitch, I'm going to kill you."

The other Syracuse offensive linemen, Gene Stancin, Dick Feidler, Walt Sweeney, and John Mackey also had a good game. And Ernie Davis, the Heisman Award winner that year, had one of his best games of the year. We beat Pitt 28-9. The game meant a lot to us for it was essentially the same Pitt team that had broken our 16 game unbeaten streak the year before.

Throughout my junior year, I continued to play tough, hard-hitting, fanatical football. The coaches continued to hold me up as a model to other players. Yet, like so many other ball players, my "courageous" behavior was often not voluntary.

Although I played time and again with injuries, and told myself I was doing this because it was in the best tradition of the game, it was really to get approval from the coaches. It would have taken real courage to tell the coach I was hurt and wouldn't play until my injury healed properly. The team physician at Syracuse, Dr. Clyde Barney, didn't make this easier. There was a rumor around that Dr. Barney had once been head of Walter Reed

Hospital, and it was claimed he had been a great surgeon during World War I.

Dr. Barney treated me often, but the time I still remember most vividly was when I hurt my elbow during practice. I'd had a poor game the week before, and at Monday's practice I was determined to show I hadn't lost my hustle. I started to put on one of my fanatical shows, which I did periodically during my junior year to convince myself and everyone else that I hadn't lost my psych.

We were doing a drill on the reaction blocking machine. When it was my turn I blasted the machine with my forearm as hard as I could, and shattered the metal piece holding the pad. The jagged metal stuck into my elbow. I was bleeding so profusely that the trainers could see it was too serious for them to treat; they sent me into the locker room to see Dr. Barney. When he saw my arm covered with blood, Dr. Barney's comment was "Looks like you got a little cut there, Dave. Jump up here and I'll sew it up." I lay down on the training table and watched him get ready. He took the cover off the pan of medical instruments and I could see all the fluid had evaporated, leaving the instruments stuck in the residue in the bottom. Dr. Barney managed to pry out a probe with his fingers and then began using it to dig out a needle holder. When he finally pried it loose it popped out and flew half way across the room. He picked it up off the floor, took out a spool of surgical thread and threaded a needle, and then began to sew up the two inch gash open to the bone in my elbow. Without anesthetic, he put in about ten stitches, put on a bandage and sent me back out to practice.

My arm became progressively more painful and began to swell up as the week wore on. I continued going to regular practices and, after putting a little extra padding on my arm, I played in the Nebraska game on Saturday. On the plane back to Syracuse after the game my elbow really began to throb. I took my belt off and tied it around the post that holds up the luggage rack, hooking my wrist in my belt so my arm would stay elevated above my head. The pain eased somewhat and I rode like this all the way from Nebraska to Syracuse.

By Monday my arm had swollen to twice its normal size. It was all puffy and felt like a piece of rotten wood. During Chemistry lab it hurt so badly I excused myself and went down to the training room where one of the trainers took off the bandage and found my arm was so swollen that the wound had opened despite the stitches and was draining pus and blood. He sent me over to the infirmary. I was getting feverish by this time, and the nurses put me in bed as soon as I arrived. Dr. Barney came in to look at my arm and told me I probably had an infection. He put me on penicillin and told the nurses to hot pack my arm 24 hours a day. He then took a culture of the wound.

Dr. Barney stopped in the next day to tell me how fortunate I was. "Listen, you're lucky that we have antibiotics. In the First World War when a guy got an infection like this I had to slice his arm like a rubber tree to let the pus drain out." When the culture he had taken Monday came back late in the week, Barney informed me that the particular strain of staphylococcus I had was resistant to penicillin—the drug he'd had me on all week.

One of the justifications for college football is that it

is not only a character-builder, but a body-builder as well. This is nonsense. My experience with Dr. Barney was just an especially grotesque example of something that happens all the time. Young men are having their bodies destroyed, not developed. As a matter of fact, few players can escape from college football without some form of permanent disability. During my four years I accumulated a broken wrist, separations of both shoulders, an ankle that was torn up so badly it broke the arch of my foot, three major brain concussions, and an arm that almost had to be amputated because of improper treatment. And I was one of the lucky ones.

When a player is injured, he is sent to the team physician, who is usually more concerned with getting the athlete back into action than anything else. This reversal of priorities leads to unbelievable abuses. One of the most common is to "shoot" a player before a game to numb a painful injured area that would normally keep him out of action. He can play, but in so doing he can also get new injuries in that part of his body where he has no feeling.

When I spoke to a group of athletes at the University of California in the Spring of 1970, Jim Calkins, co-captain of the Cal football team, told me that the coaching staff and the team physician had put him on anabolic steroids. Both assured him such drugs would make him bigger and stronger, and this is true. But they didn't bother to tell him that there are potentially dangerous side-effects. "I gained a lot of weight like they told me I would, but after a month or so, those steroids really began to mess me up," Jim told me. "I went to the team physician and he admitted that there are possible dangers. I had complete faith in the coaches and medical staff before this, and I felt betrayed." And well he might, because steroids are known to have caused atrophied testes, blunting of sex drives, damage to liver and glands, and some physicians believe they are the causal agent for cancer of the prostate. And they are widely used.

The violent and brutal player that television viewers marvel over on Saturdays and Sundays is often a synthetic product. When I got to the National Football League, I saw players taking not only steroids, but also amphetamines and barbiturates at an astonishing rate. Most NFL trainers do more dealing in these drugs than the average junky. I was glad when Houston Ridge, the San Diego Chargers' veteran defensive tackle, filed a huge suit last spring against his club, charging them with conspiracy and malpractice in the use of drugs. He charged that steroids, amphetamines, barbiturates and the like were used "not for purpose of treatment and cure, but for the purpose of stimulating mind and body so he (the player) would perform more violently as a professional . . ."

I don't mean that players are given drugs against their will. Like Calkins, most players have complete trust in their coaches and team doctors and in the pattern of authority they represent. Associated with this is the atmosphere of suspicion which surrounds any injured player unless his injury is a visible one, like a broken bone. Coaches constantly question the validity of a player's complaints, and give him the silent treatment when he has a "suspicious" injury. The coaches don't say, "We think you're faking, don't you want to play football?" They simply stop talking to a player and the message comes across very clearly. Most players want and need coaches' approval, especially when they are injured and can't perform, and it really tears them up when the coach won't even speak to them. This is especially true in college where the players are young and usually identify closely with the coach. After a few days of this treatment, many players become frantic. They will plead with the team physician to shoot them up so they can play. The player will totally disregard the risk of permanent injury.

Coaches love to recount examples of players who have played with serious injuries. Ben's favorite story was about Jim Ringo. According to Ben, Ringo played one game his senior year with infected boils covering both legs. Ben would emphasize that both Ringo's legs were covered with pus and blood when he came into the locker room at half time. According to Ben, Ringo did not once speak of the pain. He simply bandaged the draining boils, put on a clean pair of pants and went back out to play a great second half. It's like the fictional American soldier played by John Wayne who fights on with crippling, fatal wounds. In the Catch-22 world of football, as in war, this passes for reasonable behavior.

7

BY THE NOTRE DAME GAME—the next to the last game of my junior year—my infected elbow had finally healed enough so I could play. We had a 6 and 2 record and it was a big game for us because word was out that if we beat Notre Dame and won our last game against Boston College we would get a major bowl bid. We pushed them around all afternoon, but because of a few bad breaks and penalties we were only leading 15-14 in the closing minutes of the fourth quarter. All afternoon the head lineman had been giving us a hard time. He refused to talk to Bob Stem, our defensive captain, and threatened us with a 15 yard penalty when Stem tried to ask him about a questionable call early in the game. We felt we were getting a bad time because the official was from the Midwest and we were an Eastern team.

Notre Dame had the ball during the last few minutes and we were fighting to protect our one point lead. We held them without much trouble and then, with three seconds left to play in the game, they lined up for a desperation field goal attempt. The ball was on our 39 yard line, and—given the ten extra yards from the goal line to the goal posts and the seven yards from the center to the holder—the Notre Dame kicker would have to kick the ball more than 55 yards and still have it high enough to clear the goal post. There was simply no chance of this and, looking back on it, I know the best thing we could have done would have been to just stand there, watch him kick it, and let the time run out. Instead in typical Syracuse fashion, the coaches sent in the word to try and block it. Walt Sweeney, our defensive end, got by his man and into the backfield. He slammed into the kicker after the ball was already in the air. The head lineman came running up and threw his flag, calling a personal foul on Sweeney. The clock had run out and the game was supposed to be over, but the ball was moved up 15 yards to our 24 and it was ruled that Notre Dame had one more play. With no time left in the clock they once again lined up for a field goal. Their kicker got off the longest field goal of his life and Notre Dame won the game 17-15. As pandemonium broke loose, we stood there stunned and then walked off the field in a daze. The coaching staff never had a word of criticism for Sweeney even though he lost us the game. They didn't want to do anything to discourage his kind of aggressive play.

The following morning the papers reported that the official admitted he had made a mistake in allowing Notre Dame the extra play. The N.C.A.A. rule at that time was that the offensive team is not entitled to an extra play if a defensive player commits a foul and time has run out. During a Monday afternoon team meeting Ben told us he had been notified that Notre Dame would concede the game to us and let the score stand at 15-14, Syracuse's favor. But as the week dragged on, no official announcement was forthcoming. Father Hesburgh, the President of Notre Dame and noted civil libertarian, was the only man who had the authority to concede victory to us, and he made no comment. Eventually some lower-level Notre Dame administrator announced they would not concede the game, which was no surprise to those of us who had already seen that ordinary ethics didn't apply on the football field.

When we were preparing for our last game, which was against Boston College, Ben made a big point of telling us that Boston, like Notre Dame, was a Jesuit school, implying that we should conduct a vicarious pogrom on them. At one pep talk before the game he said, "Boys, Boston College is the Notre Dame of the East, let's just give 'em a little extree." Extra, pronounced ex-tree, was the word Ben used when he wanted us to pull out all stops and really put it to a particular team. But a lot of guys were pissed off and disillusioned after the Notre Dame affair and, despite Ben's rather crude attempt to psych us, we just couldn't get up for the game. All we wanted at this point was for the season to end.

Though we were supposed to be a superior team and were heavily favored, we just barely managed to beat Boston College. We celebrated after the game, not so much because we had won, but because the weight and pressure of a particularly rough season was behind us and we were looking forward to a return to normal life. No such luck: a few days later the Syracuse athletic department and the college administration announced that the team had accepted an invitation to play in the Liberty Bowl. Even

then, straight as I was, my first reaction was that the
coaches and administrators should play the game since
they had accepted the invitation. This game, which was
played in Philadelphia in the middle of December, was at
best second-rate, and all it meant to most of the players
was another couple of weeks of practice. But it was quite a
profitable venture for the athletic department. The game
was nationally televised, and even though both the
teams—Syracuse and Miami—were mediocre they were invited because each had one of the country's most exciting
players—our Ernie Davis and Miami's quarterback George
Mira, one of the top passers in the history of college football. The Syracuse athletic department would get a significant amount of the television money and they weren't
about to pass this up simply because the players were
tired.

Many of us felt that since we had to play we should
at least get something out of it. After speaking to Ben,
Dick Easterly, one of the co-captains, informed us there
were no plans to give the players anything. This made us
even more angry, because we knew that players in the
major bowls always received a wristwatch, a set of luggage or something like that. We were in a murderously
petty mood, and had a special team meeting without the
coaches to discuss what we should do. Some of the seniors
favored boycotting the game unless the athletic department at least gave us a watch, and we decided to send the
co-captains to Lew Andreas, the athletic director, to tell
him this.

The athletic department had never seen the ball players get together on their own before and this, coupled with

the talk of boycott, made them quickly agree to give us watches—and before the game as we had demanded. That was a good lesson: one of the greatest absurdities in the football mythology is that the players' interests are identical with those of coaches and administrators.

I can't remember very much about the actual Liberty Bowl game except that it was a freezing cold and windy day, and I wasn't very anxious to hit or be hit by anyone. Ernie Davis had a tremendous afternoon and almost single-handedly won the game for us. Whenever we were in a crucial situation and needed yardage, Ernie got it. After the game the players from both teams were given small metal replicas of the Liberty Bell but they didn't matter too much. Our only victory was the watches. On the flight back to Syracuse, all the players were talking about how smart we'd been to get organized and make our demands *before* the game.

8

AFTER THE SEASON I began to think a lot about what the football program at Syracuse meant. The whole Liberty Bowl experience had made me realize the blatantly commercial nature of college football and see that the players had picked up these petty, small-minded values. But it was also clear that I was basically just a hired hand brought in from Ohio, and that if I began to question the values behind the game very loudly, I'd quickly find myself back in Solon. We were semi-professionals, and the only reason the N.C.A.A. regulated scholarship money was to keep our wages down. We were a cheap labor pool that made great profits for the university while we were constantly told to be grateful for the opportunity we were getting. Still, standing out there like the pot of gold at the end of the rainbow, was the incentive of pro ball which helped keep the players from griping too loud or really organizing.

You hear a lot about how football scholarships allow poor kids to attend college. This may be true, but it isn't anything to be proud of. It's pretty obvious that this country could, if it wished, give everyone a chance to go to college. Actually, people should feel guilty rather than chauvinistic and elated when they see a scholarship awarded to a student who can throw a football 60 yards while one of his classmates with good grades who sincerely wants to attend college cannot do so for financial reasons.

It's not surprising that vast numbers of poor kids, black and white, throughout the country spend an inordinate amount of time and energy on athletics. Thousands upon thousands of them turn out for high school football every year, filled with dreams of gridiron glory and hopes of a college scholarship and immortality as a pro. Instead of talking honestly, most high school coaches play cynically upon these dreams and hopes. A study done in 1969 by the Big Eight Conference, which was published in the N.C.A.A. *News*, presents a sobering reality: only one out of every 30 high school football players ever gets a chance to play college ball. Most likely, fewer than one in a hundred get a full athletic scholarship.

But the most staggering irony is that the greatest disservice is often done to athletes who *do* get the scholarships. Syracuse did give "certificates of attendance" to the large number of players who put in their four years of football, but did not earn degrees. Apologists for the game claim that spending a few years in a college environment is beneficial whether or not the athlete receives a degree. When I hear this I always remember a guy I'll call Randy Peters, a player at Syracuse who became notorious as a vicious jock off the field as well as on. When he got drunk and walked into a fraternity party or a bar, the effects would be something like the entrance of King Kong. Despite his reputation, I found Randy a serious, sensitive human being once I got to know him. He hated Syracuse University and all its complexities. He had been brought there, quite simply, only to play football.

One way Randy would take out his frustration was by going to a bar with some other football players and "cleaning it out." They would get juiced up, drive to one of the local hangouts, drink some more, and start their routine: first they'd knock each other around, and then they'd start on some of the patrons. The people in the bar would catch on and before long the bar would be empty. Every now and then they'd meet a group of guys who weren't intimidated and all hell would break loose. Once the fight was on in earnest Randy really got it on. While he was only an average football player, Randy was probably the greatest street fighter in the history of Syracuse. His barroom exploits are now so intermixed with legend that it's difficult to tell which Randy Peters stories are really true.

Perhaps the most famous tale about Randy concerns the night he tangled with a skilled swordsman. Randy had really tied one on one Saturday night after a game, and he went out looking for a party he'd heard about. The party was to be in a large apartment house and the people who told him about it had given him the wrong apartment number. Randy knew no one liked to let him into parties when he was drunk, so he immediately began banging on the door demanding to be let in. It was about midnight and Randy's pounding and shouting woke the occupant of the apartment, a well-known Syracuse surgeon who was also a champion fencer. Randy grew more and more furious by the minute. In fact he became so angry that the doctor was afraid to open his door even after he realized Randy was only looking for a party elsewhere in the apartment building. Randy kept pounding and screaming about cracking heads, and finally began to chop his way through the door using nothing but his hands and feet. It took him less than a minute to get through—just enough time for the doctor to grab one of his swords. In telling friends about this, Randy said he would have left peacefully as soon as he saw there was no party if some madman hadn't been swinging a sword at him. It is understandable that the doctor tried to defend himself, but, knowing Randy, I could also understand why he wouldn't back down from a 165 pound man even though he was wielding a sabre. The doctor held Randy at bay for a while, slicing him pretty good in the process. But, like Rocky Marciano, Randy would take ten blows to get in one. When he did get to the doctor, he wrestled the sword from him and then broke both his hands. Commenting on this later, Randy reportedly said, "I wanted to make sure he didn't attack any more innocent people."

On this occasion, as on many others, the athletic department came to Randy's rescue and kept him out of any serious legal trouble. Randy was by no means the only football player the athletic department had to bail out. In fact, one of its main functions, second only to keeping football players eligible by any means necessary, was to keep guys out of jail. Those who were so bad that they couldn't be controlled were advised to join the service for anything from a six month hitch in the reserves to a full four years in the Marines. Ben would guarantee them their

scholarships when they returned, and he was forever pointing out the virtues of spending some time in the service
"maturing."

I must admit to mixed feelings about the athletic department's willingness to keep guys out of trouble since
they kept me out of jail once when the police had a warrant out for my arrest, because of my collection of over
fifty-five parking tickets. They handled the matter so well
that I not only avoided jail or a fine, but I didn't even pay
the original fines. I remember standing before the judge
trying to look humble and contrite. I knew the athletic
department had already worked things out because it was
Ben who had told me when to show up in court. But the
judge began to lecture me in a stern monotone: "The total
for these tickets and accumulated fines is over $800 and
you could spend up to six months in jail. Just because you
are a football player, don't think you can get away with
this kind of thing." He kept on for about five minutes, and
I began to have visions of myself sitting in jail wondering
how the hell I was going to get $800. Suddenly the judge
looked up, half smiled, and asked, "Are you guys going to
have a good football team this year?" I heaved a sigh of
relief; everything was all right. "We have a real dedicated
bunch of guys," I told him with all the boyish modesty I
could summon, "and I think we can go all the way." "I'm
glad to hear that," he said. "All of us down here follow
the team closely and are pulling for you." He quickly
switched back to his judge's face and voice, informed me I
was being fined $10 for court costs and called the next
case.

I was elated at getting off so easily, especially after the

temporary scare the judge had given me. But I was also thinking about how the judge had treated other people in court that morning. The shabbily-dressed defendants, many of them black, were given the harshest penalties while the more affluent looking, like me, usually paid no more than a nominal fine. With my background it was easy to identify with the poor defendants, for I knew if I was not a college football star, I would be in the same boat.

Taking care of $800 worth of parking tickets, of course, was trivial compared to the effort and expense the athletic department had to put out for many players. This sort of thing makes you see yourself as pretty important. With all the wheeling and dealing the athletic department does on your behalf, you get the feeling you're immune from normal responsibilities—which is possibly why some athletes act like animals all the time.

After years of this special treatment, ball players begin to lose sight of the fact that this immunity is only temporary. For those who don't make it to the pros, it usually expires along with their college reputation. There are few more pathetic sights than a former college football hero walking around campus unnoticed. The same university that used to fix his grades, bail him out of jail and give him money under the table has now turned its back on him. You see a lot of guys whose life actually stopped after their last college game. They hang on by becoming insurance salesmen and the like, selling their former image as a football player.

9

DURING THE WINTER MONTHS of my junior year, I began to think a lot about the dishonesty and inconsistencies of playing football at Syracuse. I was confused and quickly becoming disillusioned. Stacy and I split up; I stopped studying and nearly flunked out. I did a lot of reading—books like Ernest Becker's *The Birth and Death of Meaning*, Aldous Huxley's *Point Counter Point*, Jack Kerouac's *On the Road*—and spent a lot of time in bars talking with friends and getting drunk. It was really a low point in my life. By the time spring practice began, I had no desire to be a fanatical hitter any longer. Mr. Davidson, who had been transferred by his firm to the Syracuse area, came out to spring practice one day. After the scrimmage, he looked at me with something like contempt and said, "Dave you really got *one* good block out there but what were you doing the rest of the scrimmage?" I put my head down, embarrassed. The coaches, interestingly, were afraid to ask or say anything to me. I got the word they thought I was going to break out at any moment and become a killer again. But after the first two weeks I faked a couple of injuries and rested the remainder of the spring.

By the beginning of summer, I had to decide whether

to stay at Syracuse or split from the college scene. I should have known in advance what I would do. The keystone of the football mentality is not to be a "quitter." In the world of football it's especially taboo to quit when you're having a bad time of it, like I was. To drop out would be to admit an unmanly weakness. As so often when I reached these crossroads, I saw no meaningful alternatives; I visualized my choice as either sticking it out with football or simply degenerating as a human being.

I decided to stay at Syracuse and stick it out. I could have taken six units of free grades that summer to raise my average, but I wanted to do it legitimately so I enrolled in two regular courses. Stacy and I were desperately in need of money, so I got a job working from midnight to eight in the morning loading 100 pound sacks of calcium chloride into box cars and tractor trailers. I got the required grades to maintain my eligibility and, because of my job, was in pretty good shape when pre-season drills began September 1st.

I'd worked hard on getting my psych back, and had, at least momentarily, resolved my problems with the game. Once I got myself together, I had a good year: I was selected to play in both the East-West Shrine game in December and the coaches' All-American game the following June.

For the Oklahoma game, I was selected as game captain and that made me determined to hustle and be a good example for the team all week. Halfway through practice one day I noticed two men in business suits talking to Ben. One of them pointed at me and all three were nodding their heads and I could tell they were talking about me. I was a senior, and the coaches had mentioned that the pros might be interested in me. It suddenly struck me these two guys were scouts. I was already going through practice in high gear, but now I pulled out all the stops. When practice was over I was completely drained and exhausted. Ben signalled for me to come over to him as I walked off the field after practice. He asked me if I'd noticed the two men in suits he was talking to. I didn't want him to think I put out a special effort because the scouts were there so I mumbled humbly that I had noticed them but I was too wrapped up in practice to pay them any particular attention. He then asked if I knew who they were. I began to say pro scouts, but caught myself and coyly replied that I didn't. "Well, Dave, they were two detectives from the Syracuse police department, and they have a warrant for your arrest for 55 unpaid parking tickets."

Joe Szombathy, one of the assistant coaches, approached me a number of times during my junior year and offered to put me on the regular under-the-table "payroll." Though it would have amounted to about $100 a month, which I desperately needed, I refused. I felt it would buy them even more control over my life than they already had, and I had promised myself after my freshman year to keep my private life separate from football. Szombathy was always perplexed by this. I still remember him saying once, "Dave, what's wrong with you? Other guys are always asking for more money and here you're turning it down when we offer it to you. I just can't understand you. This is the first time since I've been here that a player has actually turned down money."

I wondered why they were offering the money now. My financial situation hadn't changed significantly in my first two years, so the offer couldn't be motivated by a concern about my welfare. Then I understood: I had established myself as a top player, and won the university's scholar-athlete award in my freshman and sophomore years. This made me an ideal person to demonstrate that Syracuse athletes were dedicated, intelligent, well-mannered young men. Despite this, I was hanging around with "beatniks" and reading "subversive" books. By the middle of my junior year, even though I was producing on the football field, they could see I was becoming more and more alienated from football as a style of life. My contribution to the football program began and ended on the playing field, but the coaching staff wanted more and probably thought they could get me to toe the line once I accepted under-the-table money.

I kept refusing to take it until halfway through my senior year. Then I began to feel that whether it was $100 or $1,000 a month, nothing the athletic department could give me would make me adjust my life-style to theirs or could compensate me for what I was going through. So when Szombathy offered me the money for about the twentieth time, I said "O.K." He told me I would have to go down to the Syracuse Herald Journal and talk to one of their editors who was an avid football fan in order to get the money. The players called guys like this "jock-sniffers." They were wealthy Syracusians who would contribute to the under-the-table fund for the privilege of rubbing shoulders with big-name football players. I went down and talked with this guy for about two hours. There was never any talk about money. I saw Szombathy the following day, and he said my meeting with the editor had gone all right, and that there was an envelope waiting for me at the field house. For the next two months, until I received my bonus for signing a pro contract, I picked up $30 a week in a brown manila envelope from Ben's secretary.

In November, I got a letter from "Pappy" Waldorf, chief scout of the San Francisco 49ers, saying his club was interested in drafting me. Then at 1:00 a.m. the night of the draft, I was awakened by a long distance call from Chuck Drulis, head defensive coach of the St. Louis Cardinals. Yelling through a bad connection, he said they had just drafted me. At the time I didn't read the sport pages or follow pro football and I said, "The St. Louis Cardinals?" thinking perhaps they were a team in the Continental League. Drulis shouted, "Yeah, St. Louis, you know, the old Chicago Cardinals." Then I remembered being a kid back in Cleveland and going to games where the Browns periodically drubbed a team that wore funny-looking red pants.

I decided to stop in St. Louis on my way to San Francisco for the East-West Shrine game to discuss my contract with the Cardinal organization. Before I left, I went to Ben Schwartzwalder for the advice college players now get from legal representatives. But even though I was one of the few players at Syracuse who had started for him three years in a row, Ben had no time for me. "Go talk to Szombathy. He knows about the pros. Maybe he'll help you." Szombathy, who was touted at Syracuse as the expert on the pros, suggested Drulis and the Cardinals would be fair and generous and warned me not to come on hard-nosed to them, or they'd question my sincerity and label me as a potential trouble-maker.

Stacy and I flew to St. Louis at the end of December, and spent the weekend there. With Szombathy's advice fresh in my mind, I quickly signed the Cardinal contract. It was pretty unspectacular, even for those times: $9,000 salary and $2,000 as a bonus. I didn't bother to bargain, although I later found out that players of my ability had received much larger salaries and no-cut contracts, and had played the NFL off against the new American Football League in their negotiations. I never figured out why Szombathy counselled me to be pliable.

After signing with the Cardinals—and with the $2,000 bonus burning a hole in my pocket—I flew on to San Francisco for the Shrine game. The coaches for the East were Jack Mollenkoff of Purdue, Frank Howard of Clemson, and Ara Parseghian, then of Northwestern. Mollenkoff spent most of the time talking to the press, and none of the players got to know him. Of the other two, Parseghian came across as an articulate, enthusiastic coach completely dedicated to winning. With his handsome appearance and outgoing manner, he made a good first impression. Most of the players took a casual attitude toward practice for the Shrine game. We had all been through long seasons and were in good shape, so we felt our only job was to practice working as a unit. Parseghian, however, approached the game with the same fervor as a coach preparing his team for a national championship. He was so compulsive that he couldn't adjust to the different conditions involved in coaching an All Star team. We went along with his fanatical practice sessions for a couple of days, but finally told him to cool it.

Frank Howard, the head coach at Clemson, was in charge of the defense. He was something like I'd never seen before: he looked and talked exactly like the Southern sheriff in the Dodge commercials on television. Howard became particularly "fond" of John Mackey, my black teammate from Syracuse, because he was willing to play any position the coaches asked him to. He had played three or four different positions at Syracuse and was familiar with each one. Howard seemed amazed that a "colored boy" could learn to play so many different positions. "Mackey, you sure are amazing. I don't know where you came from," Howard would say, "but I'm sure glad they sent you." He always added, "Wherever you came from you sure got one helluva suntan."

Howard customarily referred to all his players as "boy." Whenever he saw you, he would use a double name, like Dave-boy or John-boy. If he'd forgotten your first name, as he usually did, he would simply holler, "Hey, you there, boy." No one ever said anything to Howard about his behavior because he was a living caricature.

The Shrine game officials had paid for the wives to fly out to the West Coast, but one night Ed Budde and I left our wives at the motel and went out and got drunk with Don Chuy and Don Brumm. Chuy began rapping about benzedrine. I asked him, "What's the story about bennies; do they really help you play better? We never took them at Syracuse." Chuy looked at me incredulously like he thought I was putting him on. He told me they used bennies by the gallon at Clemson and refused to believe we didn't take them at Syracuse. Brumm said he hadn't used them at Purdue either. Once Chuy was convinced that we weren't kidding him, he told us he would let us try one. "Look, I've been working for years to find the perfect bennie and I think I've found it," he told us. "I have three of them with me and I'll give each of you one before the game."

After our pre-game meal on the day of the Shrine game, Brumm and I went up to Chuy's room. Chuy had worked out this precise schedule as to when you took the bennie to get the maximum benefit from it. He had the bennies securely wrapped in a piece of aluminum foil, and just before it was time to board the team bus, he got a glass of water and set it on his dresser. We all gathered around and he carefully took off the foil. Chuy washed his down with a swallow of water and then passed the glass to me. I took mine and then passed the glass to Brumm. It was a solemn ritual.

We got on the bus that was to take us to Kezar Stadium, and as we approached the outskirts of San Francisco, I realized the pill was beginning to work. It was as if I were Clark Kent, had slipped into the phone booth and become Superman. I was tense and ready to explode with energy yet I felt total control over myself. I was sure I'd be able to do anything I wanted to on the football field. When I looked over at Brumm and Chuy and saw them smile at me with a slightly glazed look in their eyes, I knew they were feeling the same way.

The bennie, along with the excellent physical condition I was in, allowed me to play this game without fatigue. I was as strong during the final few minutes as I was

during the first quarter, and even got a number of votes in
the balloting for the game's outstanding lineman. My only
regret after the game was having signed my contract with
the Cardinals the week before. I knew that if I were still
unsigned—given the game I'd just played—I would have
gotten a few thousand dollars more in my contract and
bonus.

At the team party my body was bruised and tired but
I still felt tense and alert. Later, when I was unable to
sleep, I became more and more irritable. I went to a drug-
store for sleeping pills, but they did no good, and I was
touchy as hell the following day. I didn't know yet that
most guys who take bennies use some form of barbiturate
to bring them down after the game. Today I know of a lot
of players who are unable to get free of this pattern, and
some pro teams dispense amphetamines and barbiturates
like they were penny candy.

Though the bennie may have helped my play in the
Shrine game, I rarely used them in the pros. I wasn't so
much concerned with the medical dangers, though these
are very real, but I always had a purist approach to football and I wanted to play the game without an artificial
stimulant. For me a big part of the game was the mental
challenge. I wanted to meet this challenge on my own
without the help of any drugs.

I'm not sure if bennies really help you to play better
over the long run. Many players swear by them; others say
they simply give you the illusion of playing well when
you're not. I do know that players who use them regularly
quickly become dependent on them and many begin using
them even for practice. The use of bennies is on the rise

among both college and professional teams—and, since
bennies seem to help guys play "better," most coaches
show little or no concern over their widespread use.

Stacy and I flew back to Syracuse after the Shrine
game and I finished my fall semester. In February, when I
sat down to work out my spring schedule, I realized I had
to complete 26 units to graduate with my class in June.
Normally the maximum is 15 to 18 units, and I had to get
special permission to take such a heavy load. I knew I
couldn't complete 26 legitimate units in one semester, so
this was the only time during my years at Syracuse that I
signed up for a "free grade" course. It was a three unit
Physical Education course titled "Theory and Practice of
Rhythmics and Dance" taught by the gymnastics coach.
This course was offered at the same time as a history
course I was taking. Eric Faigle, the Dean of the Liberal
Arts College, who approved my schedule, saw this conflict
but only smiled for he knew I would not have to attend
classes. I simply signed up for P.E.160G and got my grade
for three units of credit at the end of the semester without
attending one class.

Despite this, the last semester at Syracuse was my
most rewarding—mainly because football was behind me.
I got a glimpse of what school could really be like, especially in a seminar on Education and Society, taught by
Hank Woessner, one of the few teachers I met who had
faith in the students' ability to involve themselves in serious work. Hank was the first teacher to discuss in the classroom some of the problems I had been struggling with
privately during my years at Syracuse. He constantly provoked us to question the whole concept of education. He

talked about what education should be ideally and the reality at Syracuse. I began having long discussions with Hank about my role as a football player at Syracuse and the relationship of football to the rest of the university. With his encouragement, I wrote a term paper on the role of college football in higher education. The paper showed that big time college football was completely antithetical to the professed aims and goals of higher education, saying in a scholarly way what I had been feeling on a personal level since my junior year. For the first time it occurred to me that questioning the system was not something to feel guilty about, but a sane response.

10

EVEN THOUGH I'd been disenchanted by the hypocrisy of college football at Syracuse, I felt things would be different in the National Football League, and was anxious to prove myself there. I remembered how I'd felt about Jim Ringo and now, after seven years of high school and college football, I finally had the chance to test myself against the very best. I planned to play professional football for about three years and then go on to become a doctor, completing my pre-med requirements during the off-season while saving enough money to pay my way through medical school. But this changed soon enough.

By the time school ended in late May, Stacy and I had spent most of the $2,000 bonus and we were nearly broke. Five hundred dollars had gone to pay the hospital and doctor bills when my son Chris was born. With Stacy unable to work, the added expenses of a child, and approximately two months until I had to report to the Cardinals' training camp, I began to look for work. But the summer jobs that had come so easily over the past two years were no longer available now that my eligibility had expired. I was in limbo—no longer able to capitalize on being a college football star, but not yet established as a pro.

After a few weeks of looking for work fruitlessly, we moved to DeRyder, a small town about an hour's drive from Syracuse. We lived in a cabin that Dick Feidler, a friend of mine on the Syracuse team, arranged for us to get free. I was thankful for the move, for I felt it would help me get in the right frame of mind for training camp. I didn't want to gravitate toward what Schwartzwalder had called my "beatnik" friends because I knew they would have me questioning football once again and that would be suicidal. I realized I needed time and solitude to get psyched for the Cardinals' training camp.

I spent most of my time while living in DeRyder working out. I wanted to be in fantastic shape when I reported to the Cardinals in the middle of July. Every afternoon I would take my dog Sam and run in the hills behind our cabin. For the first time in my life I was really enjoying working out. There was no coach constantly yelling, and I ran for no prescribed time or distance. I just ran until I felt beat, pushed myself hard for another few minutes and then stopped to walk awhile, beginning again when I recovered. I was doing things at my own tempo. I remember picking out a distant tree or some other landmark and running there, no matter how exhausted I was. It felt good.

Every morning before breakfast I ran a couple of miles on the stones of a partially dried-up creek because I felt the constant slipping and sliding on the stones was a good way to strengthen the ligaments in my knees and ankles. After that, I'd go through a half hour calisthenic routine emphasizing sit ups and push-ups. I'd complete my morning work-out with twenty 30-yard wind sprints. I continued to avoid lifting weights because I'd always felt that weight-training artificially bulked up the muscles. I had what coaches called good natural strength and didn't want unnecessary weight that would slow me down.

About four weeks before training camp opened I re-injured my "bad" wrist working on an old car, trying to remove a rusty lug nut with a power wrench when the wrench slipped out of my grip and jammed into my wrist. It was so painful that the next day I could barely move my hand. Stacy drove me to Syracuse and I went to see an orthopedic surgeon. After examining my wrist and X-raying it, he asked if I had ever broken my wrist before. I told him I'd injured it pretty badly my sophomore season, but that I had just taped it so I could continue playing. He said I'd apparently broken my wrist at that time and had now re-broken it in the same place. He told me the bone probably wouldn't heal and suggested an operation. I told him I couldn't afford an operation with the opening of training camp only a few weeks away, so he put my wrist in a cast and told me I could take a chance on it healing. I was scheduled to report for the coaches' All-American game the following day so I called up the game officials, told them what had happened and informed them that I wouldn't be able to play.

I flew to the Cardinals' training camp in Lake Forest, Illinois the third week in July. Immediately after I left, Stacy and Chris went to stay with her brother in Rochester.

We were just about completely broke, and Stacy's brother, Joe Kennedy, had offered to put them up until I found out if I was going to make it with the Cardinals. I left DeRyder with a suitcase full of clothes, about $10 in my wallet, and the plane ticket to Chicago that the Cardinals had sent me.

My regular salary, assuming I wasn't cut, would not begin until after the first regular season game. The only money any of the players made while in training camp was the $50 we received for each of the five exhibition games. Even if a ball player has signed for $50,000 a year, he doesn't receive a penny unless he survives the seven or eight weeks of training camp and plays in the first regular season game. If he gets cut during the season, the standard NFL contract allows the owners to terminate him immediately. Once the season begins the players are paid bi-weekly. Since there are 14 games during the regular season, each bi-weekly check amounts to one-seventh of your total salary. The player who gets cut halfway through the season after signing a $14,000 contract receives only $7,000.

Flying from Syracuse to Chicago I was feeling cocky, confident that I was going to make the team. I didn't try to hide the fact that I was going to be a professional football player. While rapping with the stewardesses I must have mentioned at least five times that I was on my way to the St. Louis Cardinals' football training camp. When I got off the plane at O'Hare Airport in Chicago I immediately noticed a group of muscular guys standing in the lobby. Their close-cropped hair and their slightly boisterous behavior made me think they were football players, and when I walked over, it turned out they were also Cardinal rookies trying to get to training camp in Lake Forest about 30 miles north. While we were talking a trainer wearing a Cardinal tee-shirt came by to pick up one of the top draft choices. We convinced him to take all of us to the camp, and about eight of us packed into his station wagon and drove up to Lake Forest.

At Syracuse I'd had little contact with most of the other football players off the field. I just couldn't get into their cycle of boozing it up, cleaning out bars, playing cards, or acting the big man on campus role. Occasionally I'd go out and drink with some of my teammates, but I always felt somewhat uncomfortable and could tell I didn't fit in. Every once in a while I would enjoy some aimless hell-raising, but I couldn't get behind it on a regular basis. Then, too, I was trying to break out of football's grip, while most of the other players were content to have football as the focal point of their lives.

Before I left for the Cardinal training camp I promised myself I would get rid of the "good boy" image I'd gotten at Syracuse and get involved with and be accepted by the other ball players. I was determined to do this without compromising my own values. Rooming next door to me on the rookie floor of the dormitory at Lake Forest College was Larry Stallings, a defensive tackle from Georgia Tech. Both of us had been drafted as linebackers. Larry was an unusually intelligent football player and had won an N.C.A.A. scholar-athlete award in college. We became friendly and I discovered he too had spent most of his college years in relative isolation from the rest of his teammates. We talked about my plans to get involved, and I mentioned that I thought this would be easier in the pros because everyone had gone through college and would be more aware of society and its problems. However, a few weeks of training camp showed us there was little difference between our former college teammates and the professionals.

Stallings was also at a critical point when we became friends. As a bright and sensitive guy, he—like many other ball players—had to choose: either begin questioning his role as a football player or become a super-jock. Larry became a starter during his rookie year and with all the pressures operating on him he chose to become the super-jock. He assumed the same role I had in my first years at Syracuse—the guy the coaches regularly single out as the model for other players. He started to demand perfection not only from himself, but from his teammates as well. He'd chew out other players for making mistakes and came close to fighting with his teammates more than once. After seven years with the Cardinals, Larry has become one of the finest linebackers in the NFL, but still I'm sure he must wonder sometimes about the price he has been forced to pay.

Stallings and I were the two super-hustling rookies at the Cardinals' training camp in 1963. Although friendly off the field, we competed fantastically in practice for we assumed the Cardinals would keep only one rookie linebacker. We had both been the fastest linemen on our college teams. Larry surprised the hell out of me during our first day of practice: we were doing ten 30-yard wind sprints and he caught me by surprise and beat me on the first one. It was the first time I had ever lost a race to a lineman. I got myself together and by going all out I managed to just edge him out on the next nine sprints. After the veterans arrived, I quickly established myself as the fastest linebacker on the team. The two qualities pro coaches want in a rookie are speed and a willingness to hit. I was playing in the same fanatical way I had when I was a sophomore in college, and this, coupled with my speed, made me an ideal prospect.

However, to make it with the Cardinals I needed to adjust to the professional style of play. My kamikaze approach to the game was an asset at Syracuse. Our job on defense was to simply destroy the man across from us and then move to the ball. We didn't play any keys or try to read the offense; it was all a matter of overpowering the opponent.

But the Cardinal defenses required finesse as well as brute strength. Players in the pros, unlike those in college ball, are pretty evenly matched physically and it is usually impossible to simply out-muscle your opponent. Consequently good defensive play demands that the players be able to quickly read the offensive play as it develops. Instead of blasting into or around the man across from me to get to the ball carrier, I was now required to "read" the movements of the players across from me on the snap of the ball. By watching the movement of specific players I could determine the nature and direction of the play. The important thing was not to commit myself before I read these keys. Since I played so aggressively I found it difficult to hold myself back, and time and again during those first few weeks of training camp I would take myself out of the plays when I would charge into my man without first reading my keys. Even after six years in the league, I still played so fanatically that the coaches asked the team doctor to put me on tranquilizers for the games. While most guys were popping bennies to psych up for the games I was taking tranquilizers to calm down. I stopped taking the tranquilizers after a few games though, for I wanted to be able to calm myself without using any artificial aid.

The Cardinals were trying me out as outside line-backer and reading the keys at this position is, according to most football experts, the most difficult job on pro defense. One of the hardest things is that frequently the man you key on is not the person you have to cover once the play develops. For example, when lined up as the weak side linebacker on the opposite side from the tight end, I had to read the play by watching the offensive tackle but still cover the halfback in case of a pass. If the offensive tackle blocked aggressively into the defensive end, it indicated a run and I would move toward the line of scrimmage watching for the halfback's block. On the other hand, if the offensive tackle retreated on the snap of the ball to block for a pass, I would step back and "square up" ready to cover the halfback on a pass pattern. These two sequences were pretty easy, and if things never got more complicated there never would have been any problem. But since the offense knows the defense is reading these keys, "key breaker" plays have been developed. For example, the tackle I'm keying on might aggressively block the defensive end so I will respond as if it is a run, while actually a pass play is developing.

One day early in training camp during a scrimmage I was lined up across from Taz Anderson, then the Cardinals' starting tight end. On the snap of the ball I cranked up my forearm preparing to knock his head off. Taz, well aware by this time of my aggressive style of play, slipped me a little head fake. I stepped with his fake and he shot around, hooking me in while halfback Bill Triplett swept my end for a 15 yard gain. Wally Lemm, the Cardinals' head coach at the time (now with Houston), was standing close by and saw what happened. Although he rarely raised his voice, Lemm was furious. "Meggyesy, damn it, you were hooked again. You can't take your eyes off the tight end. It's in your notebook on page fifteen, never take your eyes off or get hooked by the tight end. I've been watching you all practice and you just aren't reading your keys at all." What had happened, then and about eight other times that afternoon, was that I was reverting to my old Syracuse style of play. With this kind of chewing out by the head coach, I felt sure I was going to get cut before too long.

But the day after Wally chewed me out Larry Stalling, who was playing behind Dale Meinert, the Cardinals' All-Pro middle linebacker, tore up his groin muscles pretty badly. Since they had no other middle linebacker in the camp to replace Larry, I was moved over to this position. It was a great break for me, for middle linebacker was more suited to my style. I could really tee off on guys without having to worry too much about finesse or being faked out. Looking back, I realize that if Larry had not been hurt when he was, I would probably have been cut by the second or third week of camp.

Even when it looked like I was sure to be cut, I didn't let it get to me as many of the other rookies did. The more precarious my position on the team, the more fanatically I practiced. In drills I would scramble and hustle to be the first in line. I never allowed myself to become preoccupied with worry about being cut because I was confident that as long as I hustled and played aggressively, I would somehow make it.

As middle linebacker, I was responsible for calling the defensive signals. I'd call the defense in our huddle but could change things at the line of scrimmage by using audibles. If, after looking over the offense as they lined up on the ball, I anticipated a quick trap up the middle I would yell out "blue pigeon," which told the left tackle to start into the hole between the center and guard while I covered the area he vacated. If I yelled "red pigeon" the right tackle would make the same maneuver on his side. If I wanted both tackles to slant in at the same time I would simply yell "pigeon," without a color. For a slant to the outside, the call was "duck," again using the colors red and blue to signify right or left tackle.

The day after I was switched to middle linebacker we went through the team drills designed for the offense to practice getting correct timing in their play execution. In these, the defensive linemen and linebackers are supposed to operate at three-quarter speed; there is no tackling, and the defense is not supposed to put up any real resistance. But three-quarter speed was next to impossible for me, and I found myself hustling like a madman to the ball, giving anyone who tried to block me a hell of a shot.

Lemm was having Charley Johnson, the Cardinal quarterback, put in backfield shifts. The backfield would line up for a formation and then, on an audible signal from Charley, would shift to another. Though I didn't know it, we were supposed to stay in a standard four-three defense during team drills. Charley would be over the center calling his audibles and at the same time I was screaming "red duck," "blue pigeon," or whatever was needed to cover the particular backfield shift Charley had called. I was doing a good job, in fact such a good job that we were fouling up the offensive plays. I didn't realize it, but I was screaming so loud the offensive backs were having trouble hearing Charley's signals. This went on for about five minutes and I was really proud of myself, even though the guys were sniggering and pointing at me. When we had fouled up the offense about four plays in a row, Wally Lemm finally stopped the drill and came over to me. I could see he was really pissed but didn't quite know what to say, for he was hesitant to criticize me for being aggressive. "Listen, you understand what we're trying to do here," he told me. "We're trying to do some timing up and I appreciate your hustle. Just forget what you were told in the meeting this morning and just get into a straight 4-3 defense. Take it easy and let the offense run their plays. You'll get your chance to hit people in tomorrow's scrimmage."

The scrimmage was the rookies' first big test. It would be filmed, the coaches would review the films on Sunday and Monday, and make the first cuts Tuesday. That night I was lying on my bunk, getting myself psyched up, daydreaming about all the good plays I was going to make when it suddenly hit me that I was going to play against veteran pros. I remembered the first day they arrived in training camp. The rookies had all been in camp for three days, and I was feeling pretty good because neither the

competition nor size of the players was that much different
from college. I couldn't understand why everyone felt
making the pros was so tough, until the veterans arrived. I
first saw some of them when I was walking across the Lake
Forest campus on my way to the locker room. Two huge
guys (I later found out they were Don Owens and Joe
Robb) were standing in the locker room doorway. They
apparently hadn't seen each other for a couple of months
and they were pounding each other and hollering "How
the fuck are you?" and similar greetings. They were wearing standard football player apparel: bermudas, shower
thongs, and tee-shirts. Their arms looked as big around as
my thighs. I was reluctant to ask them to move aside, so I
stood there for about a minute meekly watching them, not
quite sure what to do. When they stopped pounding on
each other they noticed me waiting for them to move out
of the doorway. Robb pointed me out to Owens, "Hey
Don, look here's a rook." They laughingly moved aside just
enough so I had to squirm between them to get into the
locker room.

    Lying there thinking about the scrimmage I became
even more concerned when I realized that many of the
offensive linemen, the guys I would be going against,
weighed 250 pounds or more. At Syracuse I had played
pulling guard weighing 210 pounds and was considered
one of the fastest linemen in the country. The Cardinals'
two guards, Ken Gray and Irv Goode, were pulling with
the same speed I had at Syracuse, but they weighed about
255 pounds. Most big time college teams have three or
four excellent football players, but the pros have top-flight
players at every position. In the Cardinal training camp, I

discovered that if I made one false step I could rarely recover to make the tackle. In that first scrimmage, I also discovered that a mistake could result in my being nearly decapitated.

The scrimmage was scheduled for 10 in the morning, and guys were lined up in the training room as early as 8:30 to get taped. For the first time I saw signs of nervousness among the veterans, which made them seem a little more human. I was playing second team middle linebacker and we were going against the first team offense. On the first few plays Charley Johnson sent Joe Childress and John David Crow on some off-tackle power plays and trap blocks up the middle. Bob DeMarco, the Cardinals' All-Pro center, was assigned to block me on most of these plays. I was so psyched that, despite his out-weighing me by thirty-five pounds, I was more than holding my own. Then, on about the eighth play of the scrimmage I discovered why Ed Henke, then the head defensive coach, was constantly telling me and other rookies to always keep our "heads on a swivel," which meant we should constantly use our peripheral vision so we wouldn't get blind-sided. On this particular play the offense was running a power pop end sweep. As the play began I was watching the center and two guards, the guys I was supposed to key on. When I saw the offside guard pull to my left, I knew the play was going in that direction, and I started to slide that way and look in the backfield for the ball carrier. The next thing I knew I was on the ground, really laid out, with no idea of who or what had hit me. Next to me with a big grin on his face was Ernie McMillan, the Cardinals' 6'6", 260-pound offensive tackle. Though groggy, I suddenly realized why Henke was always emphasizing the importance of keeping your head on a swivel.

Along with the entire team and coaching staff, I saw what had happened when the film was shown the following Monday. I'd read my keys perfectly, but the play was a "key breaker" and I had been taken by surprise and blind-sided. The coach operating the projector re-ran the play about fifteen times. The veterans were chuckling but the rookies were rather quiet, for they knew the same thing could well happen to them. Taz Anderson hollered from the back of the room, "Welcome to the league, Meggyesy." I felt much better about things when later on in the films I saw myself knock down a couple of passes and make some solo tackles. Not surprisingly, I'd made some major mistakes, but I had played aggressively and felt I'd met my first real test as a pro.

The scrimmage had ended about noon. Saturday curfew, instead of being the regular 11 p.m., was extended to 2:30 a.m. Coach Lemm had also given us Sunday off to "go to church." In the days before the scrimmage, we rookies had heard many of the veterans making plans to spend Saturday night in Chicago down on Rush Street. While in training camp, the Cardinals' two favorite Chicago hang-outs were Butch McGuire's and The Store. Butch McGuire's is usually packed with the singles crowd (on the West Coast these places are known as "body shops") with a male-female ratio on Saturday night of about 6 to 1. The single girls who came into Butch's were usually working girls in their late teens and early 20s—secretaries, airline stewardesses, nurses, and a sprinkling of co-eds home for the summer vacation. The Store was similar except it had room for dancing upstairs, a live band most Saturday nights and somewhat less of a bistro atmosphere than Butch's. After hearing the veterans talk about the action on Rush Street, some of us decided to make the scene at Butch's. We all piled into a beat up '56 Caddy and made the hour drive down to Chicago. At Butch's we immediately spotted many of the veterans, but we kept our distance. It's an unwritten law in training camp that rookies do not associate with veterans, at least not until they've made the team. Rookies immediately recognize this "law" when they arrive in training camp and discover they have separate locker rooms. Despite our separateness, though, we felt a certain camaraderie with the veterans, for to the patrons of Butch's we were all Cardinal football players.

Except for a few super stars, every player in training camp is fighting for a position on the team and with it a salary ranging anywhere from $15,000 to $40,000. Many players think Saturday morning scrimmages and exhibition games during training are more crucial than regular season games. A player's performance in these scrimmages and exhibitions determines whether or not he'll make the team. For most rookies and even some veterans, one bad scrimmage early in training camp can result in their being cut. Not surprisingly, there is a constant tension beneath the horseplay and camaraderie of the players. The physical release of the Saturday morning scrimmages does little to reduce this tension, for the cuts will not be made until after the scrimmage films are shown the following Tuesday.

It was exhilarating to walk into Butch's anticipating

an evening free from the tensions of training camp. After a few beers, the biggest worry for most guys was whether they could find some action. Rookies, of course, do not bring their wives to training camp and neither do most of the veterans, and all players married or not are required to sleep in the team dormitory during the eight weeks of training camp. Given these conditions, most players who went to Butch's—after an hour or two of drinking and rapping about the scrimmage—began looking for a warm feminine body to cuddle up with for the rest of the evening. Before starting out, most of the married guys who wore wedding rings would slip them into their pockets. Don Brumm once made the mistake of coming into Butch's with his wife one Saturday around midnight, and three years later the guys still hadn't let him live it down. I remember Bill Koman riding Brumm at breakfast the following morning, saying "What the hell are you trying to do Brumm, destroy our marriages? There's two thousand bars in Chicago and you have to bring your wife to Butch's!"

But the tension began to build up again around one a.m., when we had to start thinking about making it back to training camp for the 2:30 a.m. bed check. By 1:00, we were drunk out of our minds and desperately searching for the guys we drove down with. It was usually close to 2:00 before we got our carloads together. Then we began the mad race up the shore highway to Lake Forest College. If we were less than 15 minutes late the fine was $50; beyond 15 minutes, it was a standard $500 regardless of the excuse. Given the drunken state most of us were in, it's a miracle that no one was killed during those 90- to 100-mile-an-hour runs back to training camp. A couple of guys have had serious accidents racing back to make curfew. During my fifth year in the league we almost lost one of our flankers, Billy Gambrell, when he hit a tree with his new MG about a mile from training camp.

Not everyone spent their Saturday nights in the same place as I realized after only a few days in training camp. Black and white players went their separate ways once practice was over. In my seven years with the Cardinals, I never once saw one of my black teammates in Butch's or any of the other bars down on Rush Street. Nor did we ever go to the bars in Chicago and Waukegan where the black players went to relax. During my first five years with the Cardinals, the black and white ball players did not mingle off the field even in the team dining hall at Lake Forest College. Newcomers were first introduced to this segregation when they arrived in training camp and discovered that the Cardinal management had assigned rooms on the basis of race. Besides this, blacks and whites were usually assigned to separate wings in the team dormitory. But this was only a small part of the racism that was rampant throughout the Cardinals and the NFL, although it would be a while before I would discover the extent of it.

11

ONE OF THE MAIN DRILLS for linebackers during training camp is working out on a blocking dummy about
seven feet tall and five feet around. Mona, as we called
her, is suspended about two feet off the ground by a chain
and filled with sand and sawdust. She weighs well over
500 pounds. With the other linebackers, I had to practice
forearm "shivers" on canvas-covered Mona. We'd stand
in front of her, push her away, and then, as all 500 pounds
swung pendulously back, crank up and blast her with a
forearm—five shots with each forearm. (Occasionally some
of the offensive backs would have to do this drill, and
more than once they got knocked on their asses when they
tried to hit Mona, provided they managed to get her
swinging back and forth.) I was still wearing the cast
which extended more than halfway up my forearm to protect my broken wrist, and when I hit Mona with that arm
a loud boom would echo over the practice field. I felt I had
one of the "best forearms" in training camp and those
constant booms didn't hurt my reputation—on more than
one occasion I noticed the coaches watching me with a

pleased smile. The other linebackers knew the way I was popping Mona wasn't hurting my chances of making the team and Larry Stallings used to joke that I had an unfair advantage. I was in no hurry to have the cast removed; in fact, I continued to wear it until it just about rotted off my arm.

By the time we flew to Salt Lake City for our first exhibition game against the San Francisco 49ers, half the rookies had been cut. The ax would usually fall on Tuesday or Wednesday after the coaches had seen films of Saturday's scrimmage. Whenever one of the assistant coaches told a guy to go see Coach Lemm and be sure to bring his play book, it meant he was going to get cut. The fatal phrase was "bring your play book." The coaches wanted to make sure they got the book because it contained the total offensive or defensive system the Cardinals planned to use that year. Letting an opposing team see it would have been like giving atomic secrets to Russia. Besides detailed diagrams of all the plays, the book explained that year's code for offensive and defensive audibles.

I got to play quite a bit against the 49ers because Dale Meinert, our starting middle linebacker, got "dinged" early in the second quarter. (Getting "dinged" means getting hit in the head so hard that your memory is affected, although you can still walk around and sometimes even continue playing. You don't feel pain, and the only way other players or the coaches know you've been "dinged" is when they realize you can't remember the plays.) I'd been switched to middle linebacker only a couple of weeks before and still wasn't very confident of my knowledge of the defenses, so I was terrified when I saw Dale being helped off the field. I knew I'd not only have to play, but call the defensive signals as well. Lemm yelled "Meggyesy get in there for Meinert," and I rushed onto the field and into the defensive huddle, thinking I'd give a calm, authoritative tone to my signal-calling. The other ten guys were looking at me, waiting, but for the longest time I couldn't get the words out. When they finally came, it was in an almost inaudible, stammering squeak. We broke the huddle, and John Brodie, the 49ers quarterback, had no sooner lined up over his center when I could tell he had spotted me. He knew I was a rookie, and a slight smile came over his face. He began to rattle off a sequence of numbers and colors. I had the feeling he wanted to test me and was calling an audible in order to send the play directly at me. Sure enough, on that play and the next two, Brodie sent one of his backs directly at me. I was so psyched up that we stopped all three plays for little or no gain, with me either making the tackle myself or driving the blocker backwards into the hole. I was playing with my usual fanaticism and could handle these kinds of straight power plays, but I wasn't thinking too well and if Brodie had used a little finesse, I'm sure he could have faked me out and moved through my area with little trouble.

I also played on the "bomb squad" in the 49ers game. Bomb squads are usually composed of those players who don't win a regular starting position, the ones the coaches don't mind risking for use on punts and kickoffs. The chance for serious injury is so high on these plays that they are never scrimmaged in practice. The kick-off team, the most dangerous of the bomb squads, requires nothing but a touch of insanity, some speed and a willingness to hit. You sprint down the field trying to avoid blocks and drive yourself into a wedge composed of the four biggest guys on the opposing team, usually the offensive and defensive tackles. The ball carrier is tucked behind the wedge, and they are flying up the field at full speed. There is a premium on being the first guy down the field. If you take the wedge down or punch a hole in it by taking down one or two guys, the ball carrier has to slow down, stutter step, and thus set himself up for the kill. The key guys on the kickoff team are those assigned to break the wedge, for almost anyone can make the tackle once the ball carrier is stripped of his blockers.

Once you begin to worry or even think about the possibility of an injury, your days as a top-flight bomb squadder are over. Guys who have a reputation among the players as kamikaze-like bomb squadmen—like Dan Goich of the Detroit Lions, Ike Kelley of the Philadelphia Eagles, Chuck Latourette of the Cardinals, and Mike Battle of the New York Jets—are looked upon by veteran players with a measure of awe and wonderment. It's difficult to play more than a year or two with the requisite abandon, and the turnover among bomb squadders is high.

During exhibition games, coaches regularly use bomb squads to test a rookie's willingness to hit because they feel they can teach a player technique, but he must already have an intense willingness to hit or he has little chance for success as a pro Bomb squad slots are usually reserved for rookies and younger players who haven't won a starting job, but occasionally an old veteran will hang on for another year or two by joining up. The bomb squad is a real macho test for rookies, but for the vets it's a final chance to use savvy and experience to stay in the league for an additional year or two—like a big league pitcher who develops a knuckleball after his fast one dies out.

Our second exhibition game my rookie year was against Detroit in Omaha, Nebraska. I played on the bomb squads throughout the game (and through my first two pro seasons) but the opening kickoff that day still stands out in my memory. I was lined up next to the kicker, Jim Bakken, psyching myself up for the 45 yard sprint into the wedge. I went off like a shot as soon as Bakken's foot hit the ball. I got about five yards in front of the charging wedge and couldn't understand what was happening because no one had tried to block me when, just as I was lowering my shoulder to take on the wedge, a Detroit player blind-sided me. I never saw him. He just caught me from the side and the two of us went down in a heap. But my momentum carried us forward and we took down the center of the wedge, forcing the ball carrier to slow up and begin stutter stepping. My teammates, who were a few steps behind me, quickly zeroed in on him and made the tackle. I walked off the field, my head still ringing, thinking "Holy Christ, I can't let that happen to me again. I'm really going to get chewed out in the films."

We watched the Detroit films the following Monday. The game films are edited into three categories: kicking (the bomb squads), the offense and defense. The entire team watches the kicking reel. All the coaches are present, and they take turns complimenting and ridiculing the bomb squadders. Bomb squadders learn what coaches think of them by counting how many "good jobs" or "good hustles" they hear, the two expressions most commonly used by the coaches to express satisfaction with a player's performance. If the coaches are dissatisfied with the player, the comments range from "For Christ's sake, didn't you read your play book?" to "That's the most chickenshit move I've ever seen in a football game."

As the kicking reel from the Detroit game began to run, Wally said, "I want you to watch Meggyesy on this opening kickoff." I could feel the sweat gather in my armpits and begin trickling down my ribs. I thought, "Holy Christ, here it comes." The only other times Wally had singled me out since training camp began had been to chew me out, and I was sure I was in for more of the same. The film began, and Wally pointed me out flying down the field at full speed. This guy blind-sided me in front of the wedge, and I went down like a shot. There were muffled chuckles and groans throughout the room. Two guys in the wedge tumbled over me and the ball carrier was smothered immediately. Lemm turned in my direction and said, "That was great hustle, Dave." When the reel ended and I was walking to the defensive meeting, Player-Coach Ed Henke came up beside me, smiled and said, "Way to sacrifice your body on those kickoffs. Wally likes to see that kind of hustle." During the viewing of the films, the coaches seldom praised anyone that they planned to cut, and I felt good because I knew I'd be around for at least another week.

The Detroit game also made me realize that ability is not the only thing that determines whether or not a player makes the team. The coaches' personal feelings can have a lot to do with it. For instance, Pat Fisher, now an All-Pro cornerback with the Washington Redskins, was in his third year with the Cardinals during my rookie year. He was having a rough time because he had somehow gotten on the wrong side of Wally. Wally was well aware that Pat had grown up in Omaha—where we were playing—and had played college ball at the University of Nebraska. Wally knew that hundreds of Fisher's followers, including his family, would be on hand, but he ignored Pat and let him sit on the bench for almost the whole game.

Most of the players were pissed off at Lemm for having embarrassed Pat. We also assumed Pat would be cut, since this is what usually happens to veterans (except the big stars) who are held out of exhibition games. Coaches are not anxious to have veteran ball players picked up by other teams, so they usually keep them out of exhibition games and wait until just before the start of the regular season to release them. This delay in making the cut means that it is extremely unlikely that another team will take a chance and pick up an "unknown" that close to the start of the season. There are two main reasons why a coach doesn't want a veteran he has cut picked up by another team. First, coaches feel that the player may come back to "haunt" them—if a guy makes it with another club, he will make the coach look bad in the eyes of his bosses, the owners. Second, a veteran player will have extensive knowledge of his team's offensive and defensive systems, and of its weaknesses. This is invaluable information, and whenever the Cardinals added a veteran player from another team to our roster, the coaches always had him give the scouting report when we played his old team. Just before the start of the regular 1969 season, for example, the Cardinals picked up King Hill, a veteran quarterback who had been cut by the Minnesota Vikings. We got Hill because he was a good punter and we had just lost our punter, Chuck Latourette, for the season because of a knee injury, but the fact that he had detailed knowledge of the offensive and defensive strategies the Vikings felt they could use against us didn't make him less desirable. And sure enough, when we met the Vikings they used almost the exact tactics Hill said they would. Unfortunately, Minnesota was so overpowering in 1969 that even full knowledge of what they were going to do didn't help us.

Another less obvious but equally important way a veteran can help his new team is by inside information on injuries of his former teammates. For instance, he may know that because of an off-season knee operation, one of the defensive backs on his former team has poor lateral movement to his left and can be easily beaten on down and out patterns whereas the previous year he was unbeatable on this pattern.

For all these reasons, coaches realize the potential value of an experienced veteran to the team that picks him up. But despite this value, a team will hesitate to pick up a veteran if he has been kept out of exhibition games and cut just before the start of the regular season.

After Pat Fisher was held out of the Detroit game, we knew Wally was probably planning to get rid of him. Fortunately for Pat, though, during our next exhibition game Jimmy Hill, our starting cornerback, got in a fight with the Chicago Bears tight-end, Mike Ditka, and they were both thrown out of the game. Pat was sent in as Hill's replacement, and for three quarters he shut out Angelo Coia, at that time one of the fastest flankers in the NFL. It was such an impressive job that however Lemm felt about him, it would have been absurd to cut him because any team which saw that game film would have picked him up immediately if he were cut.

Not all of our tests were on the playing field. In the Cardinal training camp, all rookies were required to sing a song of at least two verses during the evening meals. It was reminiscent of the hazing scene I'd witnessed at West Point. A few days after the veterans arrived it began: each night, three rookies would have to sing. The vets wanted us to work a little, so we weren't allowed to sing our college alma maters, the only songs they figured we would be familiar with. I didn't know two verses of any song, so I snuck over to the Lake Forest College library and told the librarian of my plight. She suggested Carl Sandburg's *Book of American Folk Songs*. Leafing through the book that evening, I selected "Frankie and Johnny," wrote three verses on some index cards and spent the next few evenings singing in front of the mirror in my room.

The night it was my turn to sing, I pulled my chair over near the chow line and stood on it as required. The squad was spread out in the dining room in the familiar segregated patterns: coaches at their table, blacks over by the windows, and whites split into two groups, rookies and veterans. A few players were still coming through the chow line as I began. Jim Hill, one of the most feared cornerbacks in the league, stopped in front of me with his tray full of food and looked up with a quizzical smile. Luke Owens and the other black ball players sitting at his table were smiling and seemed especially pleased with my

Solon high school senior, 1958 — butch wax and all

Syracuse football 1958 (going on 1925 — note the knickers). The character mentors, reading from left starting at second from left: Jim Shreve, Joe Szombathy, Bill Bell; Ben Schwartzwalder is the man in the middle, Ted Daily is to his left and Clyde Barney, M.D. is third from the right. I'm number 57, third row from the top. Gene Stancin is third from the right in the row above me; others include Ernie Davis (44), Walt Sweeney (89), John Mackey (18), Bob Stem (56), Fred Mautino (82). Mark Weber is fifth from the left, fourth row down.

Defending National Collegiate Champions

a. In a rare shooting role for the Solon Comets. I averaged about six points a game, and fouled out of every game except one my senior year. A hatchet man rebounder.

b. The East team before the 1962 Shrine game. I'm number 64. We beat the West with a team that included Daryl Lamonica (3), Ed Budde (79), Bob Vogel (73), Don Brumm (75), Art Graham (84), Tom Hutchenson (80), Don Chuy (74), John Mackey (87) and George Saimes (40). Please note the Alabama sheriff, the one with the baseball cap in the second row.

c. The young marrieds, August, 1961. Purposeful.

d. The Meggyesy boys: Joe, Tom, Dennis, me and Stacy, Roger and Elaine.

a.

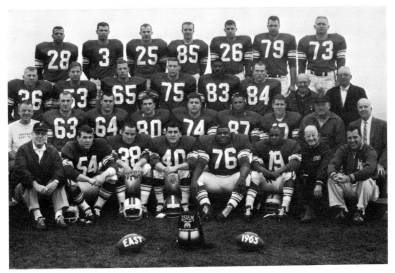

b.

Moulin Studios
San Francisco, Ca.

c.

Stevenson Studios
Marcellus, N.Y.

d.

Venditi Studios
Belford, Ohio

a.

Herb Weitman

b.

a. Jenny, Dave, Mary Ellen Flannigan, Stacy.

b. At the Washington University Library: studious.

c. The urban couple; Fall, 1968.

d. Chris, Jenny and Pappa.

e. Stacy and Jennifer jamming in Fall, 1968.

c.

e.

Featured in the Cardinals' program at the end of my best season with the team, December, 1968.

The whole crowd.

1968 ST. LOUIS FOOTBALL CARDINALS

BOTTOM ROW (left to right) -- Bill Simmons, equipment manager; Harry Gilmer, assistant coach; Dave Meggyesy, LB; Bob Lee, FL; Mac Sauls, DB; Chuck Latourette, P-DB; Larry Wilson, DB; Jim Hart, CB; Ernie Clark, LB; Charley Johnson, QB; Jim Bakken, K-FL; Bobby Joe Conrad, FL; Ken Gray, G; Dave Williams, E; Tom Busch, P-FL; Brady Keys, DB; Jerry Daanen, E; Roy Shivers, RB; Jack Rockwell, trainer; John Omohundro, assistant trainer. SECOND ROW (left to right) -- Chuck Drulis, assistant coach; MacArthur Lane, RB; Bob Atkins, DB; Rocky Rosema, LB; Walter Johnson, DE; Jamie Rivers, LB; Ted Wheeler, G; Dick Kasperek, C; Dave O'Brien, G; Larry Stallings, LB; Cid Edwards, RB; Bob Duncum, T; Jerry Stovall, DB; Don Brumm, DE; Fred Hyatt, E; Tim Van Galder, CB; Wayne Trimble, E; Willis Crenshaw, RB; John (Red) Cochran, assistant coach; Charley Winner, Head Coach. THIRD ROW (left to right) -- Dick Voris, assistant coach; John Roland, RB; Rick Sortun, G; Lonnie Sanders, DB; Vernon Emerson, T; Chuck Logan, E; Bob Reynolds, T; Chuck Walker, DE-DT; Mike Barnes, DB; Joe Schmiesing, DE; Jackie Smith, E; Dan Goich, DT; Bob Rowe, DT; Irv Goode, G; Ernie McMillan, T; Bob DeMarco, C; Mike Strofolino, LB; Clyde Williams, T; Fred Heron, DT; Dave Long, DE; Bob (Red) Miller, assistant coach; Don Shroyer, assistant coach.

Popping my helmet after a defensive series.

Verifying the pass coverage with Larry Wilson against the Eagles in the 1968 season.

a.

b.

a. About to make a tackle.

b. One on one pass coverage against the Eagles.

c. Reading the pass, but checking for the draw against the Steelers in 1968.

Herb Weitman

c.

Herb Weitman

My left wrist is still broken and tightly taped to prevent the bones from moving around. Close observers will note the "jersey-hold play" in operation.

Getting my psych up for a bomb squad run; 1967.

Herb Weitman

Some contemplation and rest before the next defensive series; 1968.

Rassling with Chris and Jenny the day after a game, doing the tickle I couldn't do the day before.

Herb Weitman

The whole family in the California sun, Spring, 1970.

a.

Herb Weitman

b.

c.

a. Getting the psych up before the Eagles' game in 1968.

b. In a heavy discussion about football after the 1969 season.

c. Writing and thinking at the Institute, Spring, 1970.

Micki Scott

David M. Meggyesy

song. When Luke shouted a few words of encouragement, even the white ball players, who normally either harassed or ignored singing rookies, stopped eating. When I went on to a third verse, I could see the looks of amazement. I gave a showman's bow at the conclusion, and when I jumped down off the chair, the squad gave a prolonged ovation.

Though I didn't realize it at the time and had simply tried to do a good job so I wouldn't embarrass myself, the coaches follow the rookies' singing performances very closely. They want to see how the veterans respond because it tells them something about team cohesiveness and are favorably impressed when the veterans respond enthusiastically to a rookie's performance. They know the veterans' response is based not on the quality of the rookie's obligato, but on his willingness to go along with the ritual.

I was feeling pretty good after dinner because of my success. I was beginning to think of myself as part of the team. When we were leaving the dining hall, a few of the veterans addressed me by my name for the first time. Later in the evening, when I was back in my room, a few of the rookies who hadn't yet sung stopped by and asked if they could borrow the song book.

12

AFTER LUNCH THE following day, there was a general team meeting. It was one of training camp's special get-togethers and something of a surprise for me because the speakers were only indirectly involved in football: they were two of the ex-FBI and Treasury agents Commissioner Pete Rozelle hires to police the players and the league. The two men were basically nondescript and I can't recall their faces. But I remember their spiel: it was a solemn sermon on the dangers of organized crime and a warning about the way gamblers work insidiously to gain information as a way of making bets—like finding out which players are injured and unable to play in a given game. The agents tried to impress on us that they had a surveillance network and extensive underground contacts in each NFL city and that we would be foolish to assume we could outwit them.

These were the men who helped crack down on Joe Namath a few years later, men who I would eventually feel were cooperating with the FBI to investigate my anti-war activities and who seemed about ready to go into the business of staging drug raids as more and more players have begun to turn on. But in my rookie year they seemed simply another symbol of hypocrisy: while they harassed us, it was more or less common knowledge that some owners bet on games fairly often.

I was on my way to my first meeting with the National Football League police force when Ed Henke stopped me and said, "Coach Drulis wants to see you right away in his room." My heart fluttered: given the fact that they were pulling me out of a meeting which they took very seriously, I was sure I was going to get cut. I remember walking down the dormitory hall to Drulis' room with the other players passing me going in the opposite direction. I was thinking, "So this is how it feels to be cut," but I was amazed at how remarkably calm I was. I knocked on Drulis' door and he shouted for me to come in. Chuck, in his gruff monotone, said, "Dave, we're putting you on waivers." Even though I was expecting those words, they shattered my calm. Chuck could not help seeing the look of desperation on my face. He continued, "However, Stormy [Stormy Bidwell, the Cardinal owner] has asked me to re-negotiate your contract." At this point I couldn't understand what he was getting at. "Since you have a broken wrist, we're going to put you on 30-day injured waivers." He went on, "If you'll sign next year's contract for a $500 raise, we'll make this year's $9000 contract a no-cut." I could hardly contain myself. In the space of one minute, I'd gone from assuming I was being cut to being offered a no-cut contract. Drulis seemed nervous about how I was going to react, but I immediately agreed and signed the contracts. I was completely broke, and would

have done just about anything to get the security that
went with a no-cut contract.

Looking back, I realize the Cardinals had decided
they definitely wanted me and, knowing my financial situation, felt that offering me the no-cut contract would have
a double-barreled effect: serving to entice me into signing
my contract for the following year, and making it very
unlikely that any other club would pick me up off injured
waivers without knowing the seriousness of my injury
since they too would have to honor my no-cut contract.
This was important because the Cardinals wanted to have
access to me whenever they needed me during the season.
If I were not picked up after the 30 days I would be placed
on the Cardinals' cab squad, where I could practice with
the team and be moved to the active roster when they
needed me.

I left Drulis' room feeling ecstatic and caught only
the end of the meeting with Rozelle's security agents.

We had a short scrimmage during practice that afternoon and I really had a good day. That evening, Larry
Stallings said, "You really look happy. You really had a
great practice out there today." I told him I had re-negoti-
ated my contract and Drulis had given me a no-cut. Later
on, I went down the hall to the pay phone and called Stacy
in Rochester. We were both excited because this meant
we'd have some money coming in for at least a year. I told
her to start getting things ready for the move to St. Louis,
and that I would try to get back before the season started
so she and Chris wouldn't have to drive out alone.

The next exhibition game was against the Bears in
Chicago. Though I was on injured waivers and could no

longer play, I still felt like part of the team since I was
practicing with them every day. And, since none of the
coaches said anything to the contrary, I suited up for the
game. I wanted to continue being part of the team, and
also feared that if I didn't suit up, the coaches would sus-
pect I had a bad attitude. I came out with the team and
warmed up just as if I were going to play. I exchanged
greetings with Roger Davis, one of the Bears' offensive
guards who was from my home town and was an All-
American on the Syracuse National Championship team
when I was a freshman.

Just as the game was about to begin, Drulis spotted
me pacing along the sideline with the other players. He
became nervous when he saw that I was excited and ready
to play. Drulis lectured me in a stern but kind manner,
"Now listen, Dave, if some coach should accidentally try to
send you into the game, for God's sake, don't go in."
Knowing how fanatical I sometimes became, he continued,
"Do you understand? You're on waivers and aren't officially on the squad. If you ever run on the field during the
game we'll be in serious trouble with the commissioner."
Drulis was still nervous when he walked away, for he could
tell his message hadn't really registered with me. I was
eager to play, and if the coach had yelled my name, I'd have
been on the field like a shot.

The last exhibition game was in St. Louis against
Minnesota, but this time, instead of staying with the team,
I flew to Rochester. My experience in Chicago the week
before made me realize it was foolish to suit up when I
wasn't eligible to play. Stacy and I packed our belongings
into our VW sedan, and headed toward St. Louis. The

rack on top of the car was piled about four feet high with Chris' crib, suitcases, and cardboard boxes filled with our belongings. Chris rode in his car bed in the back seat, nearly buried by piles of clothes and pots and pans, and my dog Sam rode on the floor under Stacy's feet. We looked, and in some ways felt, like Steinbeck's Okies going West to seek their fortune. Things have changed for the better for the players since that time, but this is still closer to the experience of most rookies than the swirl of gilt-edged notoriety that accompanies an O. J. Simpson into camp.

13

We hadn't been in St. Louis more than a few weeks when Stacy was invited to a party for the players' wives at the home of Judy Randle whose husband, Sonny, was the Cardinals' All-Pro split end. Stacy was nervous about going, and just after she arrived, she noticed that none of the black players' wives were there. When she asked Judy Randle why this was so, she got icy silence as an answer; and since she feared it might cause some problems for me, she decided not to press the point. But the other wives stayed away from Stacy for the rest of the party and when she got home, I could see she was upset. We talked about it, but I was not able to shed any light on the problem.

Stacy went to another wives' party a few weeks later, this time given by Joan Koman. Her husband Bill, the starting right linebacker, was the person who had told me during training camp that I had a good chance to make the club because my competition was "two dumb nigger linebackers who are so stupid they have trouble tying their shoes." I'd told Stacy about this, so she didn't expect to find any black wives at the party, but she once again asked the hostess why this was so. Unlike Judy Randle, Joan responded with a curt, "They weren't invited." Stacy then asked, "Well, why not?" "They have their own things to do," Joan responded. "How do you know?" Stacy asked, pressing the point. "Have you asked them?" Joan answered with an emphatic "No" and walked away. Stacy did not attend another wives' party until five years later when Dee Ann Wilson—wife of Larry, the Cardinals' famous all-pro safety—had a party to which she invited all the players' wives, black and white.

My 30-day waiver period ended after the second regular season game, and, since no one had picked me up, I was formally put on the Cardinals' cab squad. All this waiver business meant little to me. I was getting my regular salary and practicing regularly with the team. The only restriction was that I couldn't suit up for the games. One of my jobs as a cab squad member was to allow two rookie linemen, Sam Silas and Bob Reynolds, to practice their blocking techniques on me. About three nights a week Ray Prochaska, the offensive line coach, would have us stay out after regular practice ended. At the time, I weighed 215 pounds while Silas and Reynolds were both about 260. Under Prochaska's direction, we'd line up eye to eye and tear into each other. Night after night we'd battle to a stand-off. To avoid being annihilated by these guys, I would work myself up to a fanatical pitch, and while we went at it like animals in a pit, Prochaska would stand there grinning. There's nothing football coaches love more than to watch two guys really pounding the shit out of each other. Some nights when we'd really get going at it, Prochaska would signal for head coach Wally Lemm to come over and watch the fun.

In the eighth game of the season, Ed Henke severely

injured his elbow and was placed on the injured waiver list, so I took his spot on the active roster. My first pro game was to be against the Browns in Cleveland—the team I'd watched regularly in high school and whose star, Jim Brown, had once been my model. I didn't play in any scrimmage plays in Cleveland, but I was on all the bomb squads. On the opening kickoff, my assignment was to block Lou Groza, the Browns' ageless kicker. It was like blocking a myth: as I stood there watching him place the ball on the kicking tee, I thought of the time six years before, when I was a junior at Solon High and Groza had come down from Cleveland to give the feature address at our football banquet. He was an established NFL star then and now he was still going strong. It was my first game in the NFL, and I was intent on knocking him on his ass—yet I felt very uncomfortable about it. Groza put the ball in the air and came lumbering down the field. My football fanaticism took over and I really gave him a shot. As I trotted off the field, I was feeling a little guilty, but I also knew my block would look good in the game films.

John Brown, one of Cleveland's offensive linemen, had been one of my teammates at Syracuse. On one fourth down, when Cleveland was preparing to punt, I was lined up across from Brown, whose nickname at Syracuse had been "Big Daddy." As we were both getting down in our stances, I said, smiling, "Hi there, Big Daddy, how're you doing?" John seemed surprised to hear anybody break the taboo and address him in a friendly manner on the field. He glanced up and I could see the look of recognition on his face, but he said nothing. Then we smashed into each other on the snap of the ball.

I finished out the season on the bomb squads and felt I had a good year. Every Tuesday during the viewing of the game films, I would invariably get a number of "good jobs" and "good hustles" from Wally. When I'd come home from practice on Tuesday nights, Stacy would always jokingly ask me, "How many 'good jobs' and 'good hustles' did you get today?" My high point of the year was the Pittsburgh game: after reviewing the films, the coaching staff gave me two "good jobs," four "good hustles," and one "good hit."

As soon as the season ended, I got a job as a medical research assistant working for Doctors Armand Brodeur and Leonard Fagan at Cardinal Glennon Memorial Hospital for Children in St. Louis. I worked at the hospital weekday mornings and took pre-med courses at Washington University in the afternoons. I was still planning to enroll in medical school after a few years in the league. Working at the hospital affected me deeply, especially seeing the dedication and commitment of the medical staff—particularly the two men I worked for. By choosing to be medical researchers, both Fagan and Brodeur had given up the opportunity to earn easily four to five times as much as they were making. The other thing that left a lasting impression on me was watching the poor women who would come into the free clinic and wait, many times four to six hours, to get medical treatment for their sick children. I couldn't help but realize the perversity of spending thousands of dollars on a football player with a sprained ankle while many poor kids were not getting adequate medical care.

During the off season, one or two evenings a week I

would go out on the speakers' circuit organized by the Falstaff Brewing Corporation, at that time a large stockholder in the Cardinals. They would set up speaking engagements for the Cardinal players who lived in the St. Louis area, paying us $35 a night and supplying us with a movie projector and a Cardinal highlight film with a few Falstaff Beer ads spliced into the action. We would usually speak before such groups as the Rotary, or the Lions Club, high school sports banquets, and Boy Scout functions. It was clear what these people wanted to hear from me and the other players. I wasn't only to be a professional football player talking about my craft, but—especially when youngsters were present—I was supposed to give an inspiring talk about sports, patriotism and mental hygiene. I had the spiel down pretty well. I had never been taught it, but it is next to impossible to play football without it becoming part of you. I told the kids they should always obey and respect their coaches and parents and to study and work hard. "Football is just like life," I would explain, "those of you who work the hardest and are the most dedicated will be the most successful. The competitiveness of football is excellent preparation for the competition of life." I would conclude by emphasizing that playing football would develop in them the right values and attitudes.

Even then, I only half believed it myself, and it wasn't too long before I saw it was absolute bullshit.

14

BECAUSE I HAD RECAPTURED some of my enthusiasm for football, my first year as a pro was in many ways very much like my sophomore year at Syracuse. But just as under-the-table payments there had started a process of disillusionment with college football, so Commissioner Pete Rozelle's decision to play the regularly scheduled games while the country was in mourning for President John Kennedy began to disillusion me with the pros. It also led me to think about the role football was beginning to play in the national imagination.

Like everyone else, I remember precisely where I was when Kennedy was killed. I was on my way to a meeting of defensive players at the old Country Day School where the Cardinals practiced during the regular season. Bill Simmons, our equipment man, had his radio on and I heard the first flash announcement that the President had been shot, but it was not until after practice that I found out he was dead. As the country went into mourning, there was suddenly a lot of discussion about whether or not the NFL would play their regularly scheduled football games. But the conclusion was never in doubt. The Cardinals, like all the other NFL teams I knew of, continued to practice, fully expecting to play our regularly scheduled game against the Giants in New York that weekend. Amidst all the gossip about possible cancellation of the games, Commissioner Rozelle issued a statement on Saturday saying the Sunday games would be played.

When we arrived in New York I was certainly in no mood to play football, and agreed with many of the other players that the game should be postponed. Many of the guys were pissed; they knew it wouldn't have been hard to extend the season for one more week as a gesture of respect. But what was most galling was Rozelle's justification for his decision: "It has been traditional in sports for athletes to perform in times of great personal tragedy. Football was Mr. Kennedy's game. He thrived on competition."

During the pre-game meal that Sunday, many of the guys were openly talking about refusing to suit up. But they were afraid of reprisals—getting fined or possibly being banned from the league. So we wound up warming up. for the game on a cold, blustery New York City day. Then we went back into the locker room and said a prayer led by Prentice Gautt. After a moment of silence for the dead President, we trooped out through the tunnel in Yankee Stadium, through the dugout and lined up for the National Anthem.

The players were pretty bitchy and they couldn't get with it. The fans, too, were listless at first, the quietest fans I'd ever heard anywhere. But I realized the power of football that day, for within a few minutes of opening kickoff they had forgotten the national tragedy and were yelling their heads off. It was frightening as hell.

Near the end of the season, Jack Drees, a CBS sports-caster, spoke about Rozelle's decision at the St. Louis Quarterbacks Club annual dinner, when awards are given to the football team. He said he felt that playing out the NFL football games that weekend provided a cohesive force, binding the country together when there were many doubts about our internal and international security. He thought the country had been rapidly disintegrating and that football and the NFL had met the challenge to pull the country together.

Drees was, in a manner of speaking, correct. And if I'd known then a fraction of what I know now, I wouldn't have been either shocked or surprised by the talk that led up to business-as-usual for the league. There is, of course, a simple economic explanation for keeping to the sched-ule: various owners would have lost their huge profits from gate receipts if they had postponed games, and I imagine CBS, which had a contract with the league, ex-erted tremendous pressure to stick to normal procedures.

This whole dialogue suggested a deeper connection between football and our society that I would become aware of later on when I became involved in the anti-war movement. By then it would be impossible for me not to see football as both a reflection and reinforcement of the worst things in American culture. There was the incredible racism which I was to see close up in the Cardinals' orga-nization and throughout the league. There was also the violence and sadism, not so much on the part of the play-ers or in the game itself, but very much in the minds of the beholders—the millions of Americans who watch football every weekend in something approaching a sexual frenzy. And then there was the whole militaristic aura surrounding pro football, not only in obvious things like football stars visiting troops in Vietnam, but in the language of the game—"throwing the bomb," being a "field general," etc., and in the unthinking obligation to "duty" required of the players. In short, the game has been wrapped in red, white and blue. It is no accident that some of the most maudlin and dangerous pre-game "patriotism" we see in this country appears in football stadiums. Nor is it an accident that the most repressive political regime in the history of this country is ruled by a football-freak, Richard M. Nixon.

15

BECAUSE I WAS SMALL in comparison to the other line-backers in the league, I always felt I should be in top physical shape. I would begin working out at Washington University in St. Louis around the middle of April, play-ing handball three times a week with my good friend, Bruce Heyl, a doctor I had met at Cardinal Glennon Hospi-tal. When the weather began to break, I would start to run, and my routine during April and May was confined to running and lifting a few weights. I would run long dis-tances on the track and out in a large field near my house. The bigger guys who could rely more on their bulk would not begin working out until around the first of June when I would already be doing speed work—build-ups or strid-ers of 140 yards, first running slow and then building up until the last 50 yards was in a full sprint. I used to do 15 of these a night.

About a month before the opening of training camp, the guys who lived in St. Louis would begin coming out to Washington University. Quarterback Charley Johnson would be out there working on pass patterns with Sonny

Randle. Jackie Smith would join them, and Bill Koman and I would work on covering the ends and the one or two running backs who would also show up. About a month before training camp opened, I would begin working out twice a day, running about three miles every morning, doing a series of build-ups and then playing handball at night. I'd run up and down the stadium steps, and end the workout with an extensive calisthenics routine and do about fifteen 30-yard sprints. That time of the year is blazing hot in St. Louis, and I would lose as much as eight or nine pounds a work-out. By the time training camp opened, though, I always felt I was in better shape than anybody else.

Our days at training camp started at seven in the morning. The dormitories up at Lake Forest College were rigged with a fire alarm. It was right outside my door, and at 7a.m. head defensive coach Chuck Drulis would get on the buzzer and ring it in different combinations. I had an alarm clock which I set to ring about five minutes before this began, so that I would be at least half awake when Drulis started the noise.

Breakfast was at 7:30, and an assistant coach would be there with a squad-list checking off each person as he came in. For some unknown reason, each player was required to go to breakfast or pay a fine of $25. I was usually so excited about the morning practice that I'd get sick if I ate anything heavier than toast and tea, but most players had eggs, bacon, grits and everything else.

Practice would start around nine, which meant we actually had to be dressed and on the field about 8:45 so the assistant coaches could give various players individual instruction. Very quickly, each of us established his own routine. After breakfast, I would buy a paper at the school bookstore, walk back to my room, lie on my bed and begin reading the paper. Everybody along my dormitory wing would take his turn going down to use the john at the end of the hall. At around 8:15, I'd walk slowly over to the locker room and begin getting dressed in the pants and jersey that I'd worn the previous day. They would be only half dry, and I always anticipated the cold clammy feeling of slipping them on. I never got my ankles taped as most of the players did, but used ankle wraps and put tape over them. The mood of these morning practices was weird. Guys would always put off going out on the field as long as possible and then generally bitch and groan about the heat.

We usually practiced in the morning for about an hour and a half, both when Wally was head coach and later under Charley Winner. By 9:30 the ground would begin to heat up. We always wore full equipment and the assistant coaches would invariably sweat anywhere from eight to 12 pounds out of me by the end of both morning and afternoon practices. In the morning we'd normally do some fairly heavy contact work, and the linebackers would spend about half an hour on Mona and other machines. During the rest of practice, we'd do timing drills and have a period of what we called skeleton pass offense and defense, where the linebackers would go one-on-one in pass coverage against the running backs coming out of the back field. We ended the morning with a ten-minute specialty period, where kickers would practice field goals, punts and kickoffs, and the linebackers and linemen would run down under punts. After this, we'd drift into the locker room, shower and dress, leaving only about ten minutes before lunch. Afternoon practice didn't start until 3:30, so we had some time to ourselves. I'd regularly sleep for an hour or so, and then read in my room while most of the other guys would play gin rummy or poker. Later on, when I became friends with Rick Sortun, the Cardinal guard who had worked with SDS, we spent many of those early afternoons talking politics. Rick, an outstanding guard from the University of Washington, was the only person on the team with whom I had political affinity.

Afternoon practice followed essentially the same routine as the morning, except the temperature was often around 95 degrees and humid. One of the Cardinals' favorite pastimes is to talk continually about the temperature and humidity. When it's really sticky, the guys personify the "humids" as the things that get to you; the things that jump all over your back at practice, that fuck you up and make you tired. Guys would say, "Today the humids are really out," and by most afternoons the humids would be jumping all over my back.

The coaches relished these kinds of days because they were under the impression that the heat helped get you into shape. So we never went out in the afternoons without our field equipment. The coaches were continually screaming at guys to keep their hats on, but one of our secret pleasures was to sneak our helmets off and catch whatever breeze might be stirring. It's hard to describe the enjoyment you can get from popping your helmet off for even 30 seconds or taking an ice cube that the assistant trainer would illegally slip us to rub on the backs of our necks. During the first week of training camp, three or four of the older veterans would be at the edge of the field doubled over with the dry heaves. The first series of pukes had thrown out all their food, but they would continue heaving because they weren't in good shape. When a player got the dry heaves, he became a joke among his teammates—practice would slow down, and guys would look over and snicker at the one in misery.

At training camp, the mental pressure is equal to the physical. One brutally hot afternoon after practice I was in the shower, really tired and beat, absent-mindedly singing "Abilene," and washing my stomach. Fran Prolsfoot, the end coach, came in and looked at me kind of funny because I was always a quiet guy and very compulsive and nervous around the coaches. I just looked at him and wondered if he, who had once played, could understand. I was feeling tired after a day of practice, and was just showering down and singing. He gave me that funny look, but I just looked back at him and said with my eyes, "I really don't give a shit what you think," and went on singing the song.

One of the worst things that can happen to a player, especially a rookie or younger man, is to get a serious injury in training. A guy who gets hurt falls behind everybody else in learning and practicing the various offenses and defenses, and is immediately ostracized by the coaching staff. Healthy ball players don't like to fraternize with an injured man either. It's like some voodoo in which the injured player becomes a sort of leper. Most coaches believe in mind over matter where injuries are concerned. They constantly ask, "How's the leg?" or "How's the ankle?' with great sarcasm, then pat the player and say, "Well, get well soon. You're missing a lot out there."

On the practice field, the coaches scream, they shout, they rant, they rave, they swear and curse. There's a fine line between what a coach can say to a player which humiliates and insults him just enough to make him work harder, and what words might make the player beat the shit out of the coach. Both players and coaches respect this subtle line, and coaches develop a talent for emasculating a player over and over again without quite killing him. The one thing that is always evident in training camp is the coaches' absolute authority. An assistant coach can tell a player to do anything related to football, from carrying dummies to running extra wind sprints after practice, and the player must do it.

After afternoon practice, the guys were pretty exhausted. In the hour before six o'clock dinner, they would shower and shave and the whites would hurry up to The Lantern, a college hang-out about a mile away, and gulp down a half pitcher or so of cold draft beer before it was time to go to dinner. After dinner, players would sit around the dining hall drinking coffee or drift over to the dormitories to wait for the eight o'clock meeting at which we reviewed the various defensive systems we were putting in. The meeting normally lasted about an hour and a half, and from 9:30 to 11:00 was free time.

Lake Forest College is a small, exclusive liberal arts college in the town of Lake Forest located at the end of the "North Shore." It has the most elegant mansions in the whole area. It's an ideal spot from the coaches' viewpoint for a training camp because it is isolated and has no night life. Since Wally Lemm decreed the towns near Lake Forest—North Chicago and Highwood—off limits, there was really no place to go. The rationale for staying out of North Chicago was that some of the sailors at the Great Lakes Naval Training Station there might want to prove themselves by fighting the Cardinal football players. And Wally, who had lived near Highwood, said it was a haven for the Mafia.

At eleven o'clock we had to be in our rooms in bed with the lights out. I'd lie in my bed with my door about six inches open to hear the coach coming by for bed check. He'd open the door, shine the flashlight directly in your eyes to make sure you were in bed, and mumble "Good night." Players never mess around with bed check because they realize if they're ever reported to the head coach for missing bed check they face—at least under Winner—an automatic $500 fine.

A guy would be in the bathroom taking a dump or brushing his teeth and you'd hear the coach open the door and holler to him, "Get to bed now, it's after eleven o'clock." But what really pissed me off in this enforced infantilization were the times I hadn't been able to reach the one phone in the dorm to call my family until close to 11:00. I'd be talking with Stacy and the coach would come down and yell "Hang up now and get to bed." It was worse than absurd. The guys being bedchecked were adults, pulling down an-average of about $25,000 a year. Many of them are stockbrokers off season; a few have Ph.D. degrees. But you find yourself reacting like a kid. Some nights when I was really digging a book, I'd turn off the light when I heard the coach coming up the hall and pretend to be sleeping when he opened my door. He'd check the other rooms and when he left the floor, I'd put on the light and continue reading like a guilty kid who sneaks a book under the covers with a flashlight after his parents have told him to go to sleep.

The 1969 season was the first one that I was able to rent a house near the training camp and have Stacy and the kids with me; but the coaches still insisted I had to be in bed in the dormitory at eleven o'clock. This meant I'd drive over to the house after dinner and spend an hour and a half or so playing with the kids, then rush back in time for the eight o'clock meeting. After that, I could drive back and be with Stacy until 10:45 when I'd have to run to the dorm and be in the sack when the coach came around for bedcheck.

In pro football, as in high school and college, the only way the coaches can establish their authority is to treat their players as boys. After I'd decided to retire, I was talking to "Chip" Oliver, the Oakland Raider linebacker who'd also quit at the peak of his career. We were talking in the Bay Area commune where he's now living and one of his comments struck me as right on. He said he'd told Al Davis, general manager of the Raiders, that he still liked football and would happily come back to play again if the coaches would treat him like a man. We smiled because we both knew this meant permanent retirement as long as he stuck to this demand.

16

ON A FLIGHT TO Pittsburgh in my rookie year, Drulis had asked me which of two Syracuse football players—Dick Bowman or Jim Mazerick—would be the better draft pick the next year. I told him I thought Bowman would be better, and the Cardinals drafted him number two, signing him to a two year no-cut contract via a beer salesman associated with the Bidwells. The summer before my second training camp, when Stacy and I drove back to Syracuse to visit my "parents," the Davidsons, I saw Dick Bowman sitting on the lawn in front of his house with a bottle of beer and a cigarette. I stopped the car and got out. After exchanging greetings I told him he looked like he'd put on a lot of weight. He said, "Yeah, I have. I'm about 260." I warned him that training camp would be pretty rough for the first two weeks, especially on a rookie. He said he'd trim down. But later, when camp started, he didn't look a pound lighter. I knew he was going to suffer, and during the first couple of weeks, Dick spent a lot of time over at the side of the field, heaving his guts out. He was finally cut by the Cardinals after about the third week, and they had to pay him off for his two year no-cut contract.

Some of the veterans were really pissed off at Bowman because what he did creates a certain paranoia in the minds of the owners, and they come to feel that all ball players are out to screw them.

I have a special reason to remember the day Dick Bowman was cut. I was resting on my bed after lunch when I heard Ed Cook, one of the veteran Cardinal guards, telling Dick that—since he was cut and didn't have to practice—he could go down to Sportman's Park, a race-track in Chicago, that afternoon and make a little wager. Cook told Dick he had a tip from a friend of his in the Chicago City Hall on a horse in the fourth race. Ed had accumulated about $200 from the veterans, and I put $10 in the pool. To convince Dick Bowman to go to the park, Ed promised him ten per cent of the winnings. He did, and that evening, we all went to bed a little bit richer.

Cook was a true veteran. He had played under Frank Leahy and was known throughout the Cardinals as the guy with the wickedest forearm. Ed had a good "heart-punch," as they say. On "C" blocks, pulling up through the hole, he would tie you up high by blasting his helmet into your face guard while at the same time he would swing his right forearm to hit you just below the rib cage in the diaphragm. Invariably, this would double his opponent over in pain. Ed caught me a couple of times with his "heartpunch" in my rookie year, and I thought he'd broken my ribs each time. But in our second exhibition game in 1963 against Detroit, Ed was playing head on against Roger Brown, Detroit's defensive tackle. Brown was giving Ed a pretty rough time. The "heartpunch" wasn't working, and during the second quarter, Ed came off the field, his face covered with blood and his eyes half glazed. The only thing he could do was to mutter over and over again, "Christ, that sonofabitch is tough."

It's an unwritten rule that if a guy gets nailed pretty hard during practice, he never says anything to the guy that did it to him. Once during my second year we were having "skeleton drills" in which the linebackers and defensive backs practice defending on pass plays against the wide receivers, tight ends, and running backs. This one morning, Jackie Smith was running a crossing pattern about ten yards deep, and we were playing a zone defense. I had dropped to my zone and was backpedaling when I saw the ball in the air and Smith flying across the field to catch it. As I came up to knock the ball down my foot slipped and I almost fell. In the process, I buried my helmet in the small of Smith's back and we went down in a heap. I got up and started to apologize to Jackie for hitting him, but he turned around and shot me an evil look, reminding me of the rule.

In these skeleton drills, the backs would flare out of the backfield going man on man against the linebackers. All the backs we had, except Willis Crenshaw, were faster than I was, so it was to my advantage to make them aware of my presence—once I'd hit them hard, they would become more cautious, which would slow them down a little. As the back I was covering started running straight up the field, I would backpedal until I saw his head turn toward the quarterback, looking for the pass. Then I'd stop, gather myself, and as he got to me, unload on him and knock him on his ass.

In my seven years of playing professional football, I never saw two football players hassle each other off the field, although they might have had three or four fights during a practice session. There is tremendous social pressure on the ball club against this kind of behavior. Indeed, one of the beliefs which sustains ball players is that they are part of the team until cut, and they realize this kind of behavior off the practice field would result in their being shunned by the rest of the squad. Three or four guys who came into training camp during my time with the Cardinals were cut within a month simply because they could not adapt to the social norms of the club.

The second year was a critical point for me. I knew I needed a lot of breaks in training camp and a good exhibition season to make the squad again. I did get one big break at a scrimmage early in training camp which really helped. When we had scrimmages, all the offensive coaches would line up right behind the offensive huddle. I was playing middle linebacker at the time, and we were going against the first team offense. On one particular play, they came up to the line and set themselves in the down position. Charley Johnson was under the center, Bob De-Marco, and started calling the signals. I happened to glance up and notice that Head Coach Lemm, who was about ten yards behind Charley, was looking at the "three hole" between the center and the guard. It occurred to me that this was exactly where the play was going to be run, and I knew the only type of blocking on such a play would be a "C" block where the center snaps the ball and fires over into the defensive tackle while the guard pulls around him and tries to block the middle linebacker, the fullback meanwhile taking the ball on a handoff and shooting directly over the middle.

Sure enough, when the play came off, the fullback, Joe Childress, went hitting up the middle behind the "C" block between Bob DeMarco and Ken Gray. I killed the play immediately.

After this, I would glance up at Wally every time the offense came up and set up over the ball, and he would always be looking directly at the hole where the play was going to be run. On pass plays, Wally would invariably look directly at the back of the quarterback or at one of the receivers, so I could generally tell it was not going to be a running play. In our two major scrimmages, I had great days. In fact, I was spectacular throughout the whole training camp. Coaches can be helpful.

Coach Drulis ran the defensive squad with an iron hand. On the club and throughout the league generally, he was recognized as one of the best defensive minds in professional football. A bad word from Drulis could result in a player being cut from the Cardinals and blackballed throughout the NFL. During a scrimmage in my second year, Dale Meinert was injured and I was put in to play middle linebacker on the first team defense. I was over-excited and immediately blew a call on pass defense. Drulis, who was standing about ten yards behind me, came up and began to chew me out. I didn't realize the error, and began to argue with him. I finally said to him, "Oh, shit." He yelled, "Get the hell off this field." As I kneeled down on the sideline, my whole body was trembling. I was aware that no player ever talked back to Drulis. Bill Koman had told me the one thing that Drulis hated most was to have a player argue with him on the field. I'd probably made a fatal mistake and I was sure I would be cut the following Tuesday. The next Monday when we were watching the scrimmage films, Drulis came to the play where I had goofed and, to my surprise, did nothing more than mention the correct procedure. But when the film was over and we were ready to leave, he looked straight at me and said, "Before we break up, if anyone ever talks back to me again, I'll run him out of football."

During this year, I also began to feel the full force of Drulis' testing system. He would tell us at the beginning of the week, "Now you've got to be like a June bride—you don't know exactly when it will be, but you know that sometime you're going to get it." This meant we had to be prepared for a written or oral quiz at any time. The oral exams were the toughest because they allowed Drulis to intimidate the rookies and younger players. A guy who didn't know every detail on his game plan or got confused would catch hell. Drulis would really make him feel pretty stupid, saying, "How in the hell do you expect me to let you play when you don't even know it here in the classroom? Now I asked you this simple question and you couldn't answer it. If you think you're going to know this on the field, you're crazy."

The exhibition game that saved me during my second year was a game against Baltimore in St. Louis which we won 30-21. I played about half the game as middle linebacker and had the best night of my pro career. Jim Parker, Baltimore's offensive guard, and I collided a couple of times. On "C" blocks, when Jim stepped around the center to swing up through the hole, he would be running straight up in the air. Because I was smaller and quicker, I could simply lower my head and blast him right in the gut—

I remember literally hitting him in the belt buckle with the top of my head. I also had a pretty good game on the off tackle plays and the sweeps. I caught Tom Matte on a sweep in front of Baltimore's bench and dumped him pretty hard. As I jumped up, I saw some of the Baltimore players with sour looks on their faces starting to rustle on the bench like they were getting ready to beat the shit out of me. If you tackle a guy pretty hard in front of his bench, you always want to avoid getting tangled up with the other ball players standing along the sidelines. Players from opposing teams who've made tackles in front of the Cardinals' bench have on more than one occasion left with kicked ribs or stomped hands.

On one play in the Baltimore game we had a blitz on where all the linebackers shot towards Johnny Unitas. I was picked up by the center, but our left linebacker went in and knocked him down. Matte had apparently failed to get off a block. As we broke from our defensive huddle for the next play and trotted up to the line, I could hear Unitas in the Baltimore huddle hollering, "Goddamn you, Matte. Don't you know your goddamn assignments?" Matte, hanging his head, mumbled something and Unitas screamed, "Goddamn you, I'm the only one who talks in this huddle, and don't you ever forget it."

Because of our 9—5 record the previous year, many people expected the Cardinals could win the division championship in 1964. We started off well, winning most of our ball games, and then the player's wives, smelling that playoff money, decided to hold a pep party for the team. The wives wanted to impress upon their husbands the need for keeping it together because of the extra thousands of dollars winning the division title and getting into the championship would bring. The party, held in the middle of the week at a motel, was something like a Tupperware get-together. When Stacy and I arrived, there were pictures of each player on the wall with play money stapled and taped up all around them. The theme of the party was up front: "We're behind you guys, and we want a piece of that championship money too." This was pretty crass, but not too unusual in the NFL: at Green Bay, it was said that each of the wives automatically received a mink coat when the Packers won the championship as a bonus beyond the money the players received.

In this second year, as before, I would get terrifically nervous before a game. I'd lie near my locker in my full uniform. I was lying with my head propped up on my helmet trying to breathe normally one Sunday before a game when I felt a sharp pain in my foot and heard Drulis holler, "Hey, what the hell are you doing? Are you going to sleep?" I realized he'd kicked me and sat up immediately, blurting out, "I wasn't sleeping." He hollered again, "What the hell are you doing? Is that any way to get ready for a game?" He was yelling pretty loud, and a lot of guys were standing around looking at me. I was pretty nervous and told him, "Listen, hell no, I wasn't asleep. This is how I try to calm myself." I wasn't playing regularly yet, and the fear of getting cut was still there. I was afraid Drulis might think I had lost my attitude and didn't care about professional football. All coaches consider themselves great amateur psychologists, and feel they can read a player's soul in his face. This accounts for a common saying among players: "Here comes the coach, put on your game face."

The coaches never seemed to realize that it was not an easy thing for guys to psych themselves up for what they had to go out and do during a game. I would spend a lot of time just trying to get my nervous system together. Other guys had other techniques. Just before we went out on the field, for instance, Ernie Clark, one of our linebackers, would disappear. The rest of us would be in the locker room, down on one knee going through the Lord's Prayer, and above our mumbling, you could hear this steady pounding noise. It was Ernie with his helmet on, beating his head against the concrete walls of the training room.

It amazed me to find out that players in other sports didn't face this incredible psychological tension. In September, 1968, for example, the Pittsburgh Pirates were in St. Louis for a game against the Cards. (Busch Stadium in St. Louis is also the home of the baseball Cardinals and our locker room was adjacent to the dressing room used by visiting National League teams). It was a week day, and we had just finished practice when the Pirate players began to file into their locker room to dress for their game against the Cards that evening. The door between our room and theirs was unlocked, and some of the half-dressed Pirates came drifting over to chat. Most of them were eating sandwiches and drinking beer, even though the beginning of their game was only about an hour off. Being familiar with the violence football players subject themselves to as a way of getting their psych up, I could hardly believe my eyes. A few of the Pirates were so drunk that they had trouble navigating around the room.

During our game against the Giants in St. Louis that year, I was on the punt team in the slot position lined up a yard off the ball between the center and the guard. Sam Huff, New York's middle linebacker at the time, was making indications he planned to shoot the gap between the guard and center and try to run over me to get our punter. On the play, he did come flying through the gap, and I let him have it with a forearm into the gut. I felt my forearm almost go back to his spine, and I remember thinking, "My God, this guy's an all-pro but he's soft as jelly." I heard his breath go out in a rush and as he doubled over he tried to grab me and punch me in the helmet. Huff had a reputation as a quasi-dirty ball player and was fairly mean, but he was never the great middle linebacker the New York press corps claimed he was. Sam was one of those players made by television. He came in a split second late on a lot of tackles, and the TV camera's indiscriminate eye couldn't tell the viewer he was mainly a clean-up man. Sports writers generally aren't much more astute than the average fan, and they were carried along on the bandwagon. This is not to say that Huff was inadequate, just that he wasn't as good as, for example, guys like Joe Schmidt, Ray Nitschke, Dick Butkus, or the Cardinals' Dale Meinert.

Much to the dismay of the Cardinal wives, we finished second in 1964, although this did qualify us for the Runner-Up Bowl in Miami against the Packers. Wally was fanatical about winning the game and immediately instituted double sessions, but after the first day he had a minor player revolt on his hands. The veterans were bitching so much to the assistant coaches that Wally got the word and by the next morning told us we could have the afternoon off. But he decreed that no one would be allowed in the motel swimming pool because he had this strange notion that swimming messed up football muscles. The Packers were in the motel next door, and from our windows we could see them swimming in their pool in the Florida sunshine and having a fine time. Some of us walked half a mile down the road to sneak into the ocean and beat the Miami heat.

Two days before the game, I drove out to the airport with Luke Owens, our regular defensive tackle, to arrange for flights back home. Luke could see I was kind of depressed, and I talked to him about the fact that I hadn't played very much that season. I told him I thought the Cardinals wanted to cut me or trade me. He said not to worry about it because anybody who comes from a good ball club will probably be picked up and he felt I could play anywhere in the National Football League. Luke warned me not to ask to be traded, because this would immediately mark me throughout the league as a "troublemaker." Coaches felt your utility, like your body, belonged to them, and that any decisions to trade you were to come from them and not from you. You are property, and property isn't supposed to think.

Some of my depression disappeared when we beat the Packers at Miami 24-17. I remember sitting on the bench after the game counting the eight $100 bills the victory had meant. I was all sweaty and hot, and I just sat there in my pads and helmet feeling the crisp newness of those bills in their little brown envelope.

During the season I'd decided to try to enter graduate school in education rather than pre-med. So I spent the spring of 1965 taking a couple of courses at Washington

University while again working as a medical research assistant and making speeches for Falstaff. Also that spring, Stacy and I attended a teach-in on the Vietnam war held at Washington University. My only previous political activity had been some vague involvement with the civil rights movement during my first year in the league. The NAACP had asked to use my name on a fund-raising letter going out to people in the St. Louis area. I'd hesitated because I thought that if any ball player should be on that letterhead, he should be a black, but the president of the St. Louis NAACP chapter convinced me this was no problem. I also worried a little about reprisals from the Cardinal organization, especially because my position on the team was pretty precarious; but this fear brought with it guilt at being so chickenshit, so I gave them my name. Looking back, I realize allowing the NAACP to use my name was the first step in my political education and sense of commitment that would culminate in my leaving professional football six years later.

17

DURING THE OFF SEASON after my second year, my biggest worry in terms of football was Dave Simmons, a linebacker from Georgia Tech, who was the Cardinals' number two draft choice and was slated to be Dale Meinert's back-up. I felt the Cardinals would now surely trade me, and I hoped it would be soon. With the competitive bidding between the AFL and the NFL, I knew Simmons would surely receive a multi-year no-cut contract, and that if I wasn't traded, I'd have a hell of a time making the team because the four veteran linebackers, Larry Stallings, Dale Meinert, Marion Rushing and Bill Koman were sure to stay.

By the opening of training camp in 1965, my fortunes looked very bleak. My contract was for $12,000—a $2500 raise which I considered significant, although not particularly generous considering the fact that I had come so cheaply during my first two years. I started out fast because I was in my usual good shape and I came to camp a superhustler and fanatic football player. Dave Simmons was down in Evanston at the All-Star training camp and would not report to the Cardinals until after the first week of August, which gave me almost three-weeks to establish myself as the number two middle linebacker.

At the last team meeting before our first exhibition game in St. Louis, while Wally was going over the details for the game, it occurred to him that this would be our first visit home in five weeks. We were scheduled to arrive in St. Louis about noon the day of the game but we didn't play until eight that night and Wally justifiably suspected that many of us would be jumping in the sack with our wives that afternoon. He was concerned that this pre-game action would sap our energy and keep us from playing good football and was pissed off that the schedule had put him and us in this predicament. So, at the end of the meeting, he launched into an impassioned speech about how we were playing in St. Louis for the first time since last season and had to look good for the home town folks. Working his way to the climax of the speech, Wally concluded, "Now guys, I know you're going to St. Louis. I know you haven't seen your families in a long time and I know you haven't seen your wives for a long time. But for godsakes guys, when you get home this afternoon, please use your heads." This literally broke up the whole meeting. Guys just doubled over in their chairs laughing. Wally, his face red, dismissed us quickly.

Throughout training until ten days before our last exhibition game up at Green Bay, Dave Simmons was playing defensive end instead of linebacker and hating every minute of it. He not only hated it, but he was doing horseshit. Dave was a great athlete but, as he admitted, one of the things he hated most was getting down into a three-point stance. He became the kind of athlete who played only at the level needed to survive in the league. He wasn't a hustling ball player, and like any other sane person, he didn't particularly like to hit or be hit. But as the pro football cliché goes, "A player has got to want to love to hit."

During the exhibition games I played very little but I did fairly well on the bomb squads. I was sure the coaching staff would eventually move Simmons over to middle linebacker and cut me, and a few days before the last exhibition game, Dave was indeed moved and I was shifted to outside linebacker. I felt the Cardinals would have made this move and cut me much earlier if I hadn't been having such a great training camp. Now I felt I'd probably be the last cut on the squad. Since I was playing so little in the exhibition games, the various teams around the league had not been able to see what I could do, so being cut would probably mean being waived out of the league. As I mentioned earlier, this is one of the ways pro clubs cut a veteran: keeping him out of exhibition games so none of the other teams have a chance to look at him. He is usually cut last, and since every team in the league is trying to get down to the 40-man limit at that point he has little chance to make it with another club.

This happened to Mike Strofolino in 1969. Mike had been our second string middle linebacker behind Jamie Rivers in 1968, but the Cardinals drafted Chip Healy, a linebacker from Vanderbilt as their number two choice. Healy was reported to be a superman. Dick Voris, the defensive line coach who scouted Chip, thought he was the Cardinals' answer to Dick Butkus; as the players would put it, Chip was "his boy." Chip came to camp and turned out to be more like what we called a nice guy than a killer. Strofolino was given a shot in the first scrimmage against the college All-Stars because Jamie Rivers was hurt, but he made a few errors and was shunted to the third string middle linebacker spot. Before training began in '69, Coach Charley Winner had assured Mike that he would play 50 per cent of the time in the first three exhibition games, but as it worked out, Mike played very little. Mike was the last cut for the Cardinals and since other teams in the league had not seen him during the exhibition season, nobody picked him up. Mike eventually went to play in Canada.

In 1965, I was confronted with about the same situation vis-a-vis myself and Simmons. Rick Sortun and I had been out drinking the night before the last exhibition game in Green Bay and I said, "Rick, this looks like my last pro game, so let's have a good time." But during the second quarter against the Packers, Larry Stallings' knee was torn up by a vicious block from Paul Hornung. I'd been playing outside linebacker for about ten days in training camp and was put into the game at left linebacker. In pro football, the coaches often tell you, "If you're going to make a mistake, make an aggressive one." So, true to my typical fanatical style, I went crazy in the game against Green Bay. I was making solo tackles in the backfield and really mixing things up and played an excellent three quarters. I also made some big mistakes. The most glaring one was leaving Hornung, the man I was supposed to cover, completely alone in the end zone to catch a touchdown pass which eventually lost us the game. But the Cardinal coaches were so awed by my aggressive play that for the next four games in the regular season I started at left linebacker.

I got a chance to start in the game against Cleveland which at that time had the greatest running back in the league, Jim Brown. I was getting psyched up all week for him, as were all members of the Cardinal defense. I knew a lot of people who had followed my career at Solon High School and at Syracuse would be at this game, and for awhile I held my own. One of Brown's favorite plays was a sweep to the strong side of the formation. On this particular play, the tight end would "tailor-block" the linebacker—that is, he would come out of his stance slowly and attempt to get the linebacker to commit himself either to the inside or the outside; once the linebacker started to move, the tight end would block him, and the pulling guards would then take the play either inside or outside the tight end's block. This kind of play developed one time and I got hold of John Brewer, the Browns' tight end. Instead of committing myself, I wanted to string Brewer down along the line of scrimmage, making the guards take the play outside, where the cornerback could handle it. On this particular play I could see Brown with the ball about even with Brewer and me. Suddenly Brown came flying up the field straight at my inside. I slipped Brewer's block and lunged for Brown, hitting him with my helmet and shoulders. I felt like I'd grabbed hold of a steel telephone pole charged with 220 volts. Brown ran over me, hitting me so hard I was looking out the earhole of my helmet with my nose mashed against the side of my face when the play was over. I had a hell of a time twisting my helmet around straight so I could pull it off.

During the second quarter we had a blitz on. As I was flying into the Cleveland backfield, I saw that Brown was the guy I'd have to run over to get to Frank Ryan, Cleveland's quarterback. I had been under the illusion, probably from reading the newspapers and listening to league gossip, that Brown was not a good blocker. (Actually, in the game films we saw, Brown did little blocking, most of the time swinging out to the flat as a safety valve.) As I went in toward Ryan, revenge was on my mind for the way Brown had almost kicked my head in on that sweep. I was thinking, "I'm going to really drill him and test the son of a bitch." As I hit him with everything I had, Brown moved backwards about six inches and I watched stars from the blow of his forearm.

Later on in the quarter, Dale Meinert, our middle linebacker, again called the same blitz. As a linebacker, you can attempt to put a move on the back assigned to you, faking him and getting ahold of him with your hands, instead of trying to run over him. Since I had tried to drill Brown on the previous blitz, I had him partially set up for a fake. As I was flying in the second time I lowered my shoulder as if to try and run over him again, and then grabbed him by the shoulder pads and spun him around. Much to my amazement, I got by him, and although slightly out of the play, I managed to get a piece of Ryan along with Chuck Walker and Don Brumm.

During the '66 season we were playing Cleveland at Cleveland and we had put in a special blitz where the right outside linebacker, instead of shooting straight in from his position, would swing around the defensive tackle and end on his side and come flying up the middle. During the game Dale Meinert had called this blitz and Bill Koman was going full speed when he hit the hole in the middle of the line, eyes closed and arms pumping. Bill was about two yards in the backfield when Brown slipped up—out of no-where it seemed—and unloaded his right forearm into Koman's head. Bill stopped dead in his tracks, sliding down in front of Brown like a steer whose head had been slammed by a sledge hammer at a slaughter-house.

Much of the talk about Brown's inability to block was racist in nature, coming from people who knew they couldn't say anything about his ability as a ball-carrier. But those, like Bill Koman, who ran into Brown, quickly found out how wrong they were.

18

FOLLOWING THE 1965 season, I got a job as program director for the National Conference of Christians and Jews in St. Louis. One of our major programs, a colloquium on how to raise unbigoted children, was held at the St. Louis Ethical Society. The assistant leader there was John Hartwell Moore. Stacy had met him briefly at the huge October 1965 peace march in Washington, D.C., which she attended along with three busloads of St. Louis peace activists. John had become our good friend, and he introduced me to a whole body of radical literature. That winter and spring I read many books John suggested and subscribed to *Ramparts, The Guardian* and other radical publications.

I entered graduate school in January of 1966 and was taking courses in the School of Education, notably one course taught by Irving Louis Horowitz, the sociologist and editor of *Trans-Action*. In response to my question about which books I should read as a background to sociology, Horowitz pulled out C. Wright Mills' *The Sociological*

Imagination and said to go through it carefully. I did, and it influenced my thinking more than any other up to that moment.

Before I left for training camp, John Moore introduced me to people in the Washington University SDS. I didn't join formally, but I attended their meetings and was sympathetic to their political analysis and programs. At that time, all the organizing in St. Louis was directed toward ending the war. One project involved block by block canvassing in various neighborhoods to find out how people felt about U.S. involvement in Vietnam and distributing literature to inform people about the genocide that was the reality underneath LBJ's rhetoric. I was surprised to find that people in the small suburban town on the outskirts of St. Louis where I lived were split almost fifty-fifty concerning U.S. involvement in Vietnam, although those who opposed the war felt frustrated and helpless about ending the bloodshed.

That year, the league expanded by giving Atlanta a franchise, and all teams were required to put a certain number of players in the veteran player pool. I was sure that either Marion Rushing or I would be put in the pool. The owners did not announce who they put in, but when the Falcons added Marion to their roster, I knew the Cardinals had protected me. This enhanced my bargaining position when contract negotiations began. I decided not to negotiate face-to-face as I had done before. My theory was that the owners played on the authoritarianism of their relationship to the players in these meetings by making you feel like an ungrateful son for not taking their first offer, so I handled preliminary negotiations by letter. It worked:

although I'd not played a great deal in the '65 season I received a $5000 raise, making my 1966 salary $17,000.

Before training camp opened in 1966, Stacy and I spent a week in a cabin on Long Island. Doing wind sprints on the beach and running about four miles every morning got me in excellent shape. Wally Lemm had been fired that spring, and Charley Winner, a former assistant coach at Baltimore, had taken his place. In a three minute conversation, Winner told me I would have to beat out Bill Koman for the starting job, but that it was still wide open as far as he was concerned. Each of us would play half of the first three exhibition games and the guy who did the best job would be the starter. Since it was Charley Winner's first year as head coach and since I felt I could make the first team, I wanted to prove myself to him. As usual, I went to training camp with the rookies in order to get a jump on the other vets. Because of my speed and because I was learning the moves of outside linebacker, I was able to cover the halfback flaring out of the backfield fairly well. When Stallings came to camp with the rest of the vets and watched me in a scrimmage, he said he was sure I'd beat out Koman for the starting position if I could keep it up.

Winner seemed much more business-like than Wally Lemm and also seemed to have a more solid grasp of pro football and a greater understanding of players. This turned out to be a facade, however. After the 1966 season, I began to think of him as a coach with little courage and practically no ability to confront football players on their own terms. I found him weak and vacillating, even in his language. One of Winner's favorite sayings was, "You've got to get over the hump." It was never clear to us what he meant by the hump, except that it was something we had to get over. Another one of his nuggets of wisdom was, "Don't cheat your body," so, especially in skeleton drills during afternoon practice, the guys would chant, "Cheat your wife but don't cheat your body."

Charley would always lead us in calisthenics and, in the morning just before exercises began, there was his "spinner." Winner picked out a rookie and had him come up in front of the squad. The rookie was told to hold a football vertically above his head, stretching his arms out and tilting his head back to stare at the end of the ball while spinning around ten times. After he was through spinning, he had to try to kick the football. This, of course, was very hard to do for a wildly dizzy man, and he would look hilariously funny staggering around the field in front of the squad, falling down and getting up and trying to kick the ball. The rationale behind this was that laughing together built up team morale, although Winner never considered the fact that being the object of senseless ridicule wasn't so amusing to the rookie he made do this "spinner."

Football players tend to be sadistic in their humor or more often just humorless. This is a shame, for there is much that is amusing. For instance, Dale Meinert, the defensive captain, was an inveterate tobacco chewer. He used to keep two discarded athletic tape cans in his locker. One was taped shut with a slit in the top. This was the "fifty-center" can, a sort of bank for the fifty cent fines Chuck Drulis assessed those who made mistakes during his oral quizzes. The other was Dale's tobacco juice can. He chewed continually during our evening meetings and every once in a while, you'd hear a plop from the back of the room where Dale was spitting a wad into his tobacco juice can. Now and then, especially during the game films when the lights were out, somebody would accidentally kick his can over, spreading a smelly dark-brown pool around Dale's chair. When the juice reached other players' bare feet they would jump up and start screaming like madmen.

But the funniest player on our team, at least for me, was our fullback, Willis Crenshaw. Willis had this image of himself as Mr. Wonderful, the man who was adept at everything, especially if it was "in." For instance, he got heavily into karate for a while and actually became quite good. I had him perform for a group of high school students when I was program director for the National Conference of Christians and Jews, and he did the brick-breaking routine. But Willis insisted that he, like James Bond, was really deadly. Then in a game against the Bears, Joe Fortunato, Chicago's notoriously tough linebacker, began to give him a hard time. Willis warned Fortunato what was going to happen if he didn't watch it, and the next time they tangled, Willis stepped dramatically back into his karate stance. In an instant, Fortunato had blasted him on the chin a couple of times and Willis was lying on his back.

Willis was a gambler too, a sort of self-styled Nick the Greek, and he was always the biggest loser in the card games that went on eternally in the Cardinals' dormitory at Lake Forest. It got so bad that when people needed a little extra money they'd go looking for Willis and get up a card game. Still, Willis thought he could bet and win on anything. Though he wasn't very fast he used to ride Fred Heron, a defensive tackle, about being slow. Willis finally said he'd spot Freddy five yards and race him in a 100-yard dash. Word got around and by the day of the race, there were hundreds of dollars riding on the outcome. Willis lost by ten yards. Another time Willis found out one of the rookies, Mike Campbell, was a former lifeguard and swimmer, so of course Willis challenged him to a duel to see who could hold his breath longest under water. They jumped in the Lake Forest swimming pool simultaneously, and after 30 seconds or so, Willis surfaced, blowing and spluttering and asking, "Where is he? Where is he?" Campbell was under water where he stayed for another minute and a half while Willis was getting out of the pool, grabbing a towel and drying himself off.

But some of the humor was more poignant. I remember getting a special kick out of one episode which involved one of the maids at training camp. She was about 35, white, and fond of one of the black players. One of the coaches who was especially down on blacks got her alone to chastize her and also intimate that he would be a more fitting recipient for her affections. The maid accommodated the coach and promised to be faithful to him. But she was actually deceiving the coach with the connivance of the black player. As he told me later, he was often performing coitus with this woman only an hour or so before the white coach would practice cunnilingus on her.

But during 1966 I didn't find much of anything very funny. This first training camp under Winner was the

roughest I'd been through in my four years in the league.
But he did keep his pre-season promise, and I was playing
half of each exhibition game alternating with Bill Koman
at right linebacker. When we faced Detroit I was feeling
fairly well, but on an off-tackle power play aimed directly
at me it looked as though I had ducked a tackle—which I
had to some extent. I rarely missed a tackle when I was
playing pro ball, but when I did it usually was because of
a fear of getting my head kicked in. I always tried to psych
myself out of this fear but sometimes it refused to get
psyched away and I would find myself turning my face
away from a ball player's driving knees. After missing the
tackle on this particular play, I became rattled and made a
couple of other errors.

Chuck Drulis then got on me and began to chew me
out at half-time. He said I was "afraid to stick my nose in
there," as he always put it, adding that I looked "almost
feminine" in making the tackle. This sort of attack on a
player's manhood is a coach's doomsday weapon. And it
almost always works, for the players have wrapped up
their identity in their masculinity, which is eternally precarious for it not only depends on not exhibiting fear of
any kind on the playing field, but is also something that
can be given and withdrawn by a coach at his pleasure.
Most coaches—Vince Lombardi was the classic example—
give their players a tantalizing hint of what it might be
like to be a man, but always keep it just out of reach.
That's why the major motif of *Instant Replay* is Jerry

Kramer's constant worry about what Lombardi is thinking of him. What is striking about the relationship is Kramer's obvious inability to deal with the man and his need to build him into an epic father-figure.

The sex thing in pro football is strange. One year the word was out around the league that homosexuality was fairly open in one NFL locker room. One veteran of that team told me that those players who were "in on the program" would stay after practice until all the straights had left and then do their thing. According to this player, about 15 of his teammates were involved.

This is a fairly extreme instance but it confirms my general impression about football players: although they have an image as super-masculine males, they are actually quite conventional, almost repressed, in their behavior. Ball players, like beer salesmen and advertising executives, talk continually about sex, about the need to get laid and how they themselves almost got laid quite recently. But when there is an actual possibility that something will happen, I've noticed that football players work up to approaching a woman just the way they work themselves up into playing. They range somewhere between boyish shyness and a heavy-handed caricature. In Butch McGuire's and other Cardinal hangouts, I remember my teammates coming on to women like Al Capone's heavies, with lines like "Hey, baby, wanna make it tonight?"

Some players do have women they see regularly in various road towns and these women are discussed quite openly. But all the talk is enveloped in a puritanical view of sex and an insistence on the double standard: wives are virginal creatures keeping the home and the kids; other women are meat on the rack.

The way they talk, players seem to see sex as something close to athletics. That is, they worry a lot about "staying power" and "performance" and dream of being able to inspire a string of orgasms in a woman the same way they dream of single-handedly making a long series of tackles. I've always been struck by the fact that football is filled with language that is heavily sexual: "hole," "hitting the hole," "sticking it in there," "thrusting ahead," and all the rest. Using his body as a weapon in the game seems to carry over in the player's private imagination. On the Cardinals, for instance, we had a player who would talk eagerly about returning to see his wife when we'd been away for a while. When he was about ready to leave for home, he'd invariably say "I'm really going to punish the old lady tonight."

After Drulis dressed me down for ducking the tackle, Bill Koman started in the second half and played the third quarter of the Detroit game, while I returned for the fourth quarter. I had calmed down by then and played well, but the missed tackle left an impression of failure on my mind. After the game, I was supposed to go out with some of the other players to a place called the Rooster Tail where a lot of young hip Detroiters hung out, but I went back to the hotel instead. I remember sitting on my bed and being seriously depressed. I knew I'd blown my chance to be number one linebacker and I couldn't figure out why. I began to seriously doubt my ability to play professional football, chastizing myself as a chicken-hearted bastard, and seriously considered jumping out of my twelfth story window.

Almost a year passed before I began to gain some insight into why I made the mistakes I did in that particular ball game and in others. I was reading White's *Streetcorner Society* one afternoon in the library at Washington University and came upon a description of an excellent baseball player who would invariably make mistakes when he played with his gang. In the gang's nonathletic pecking order, he was about in the middle, and whenever he played baseball, he would always subconsciously sabotage his efforts so as not to look better than the gang leader and cause a crisis. I began to think about my relationship with Bill Koman and about his relationship with the rest of the team. All members of the Cardinals recognized Bill as one of the leaders. He could hold sway in social situations because of his quick wit and vitriolic tongue, and he was part of the elite which initiated rookies into the organization and set the Cardinals style off the field. It occurred to me that the same kind of social pressures that had been operating on White's baseball player were probably operating on me. Deep down I felt I couldn't possibly beat out Bill Koman, although I and other players knew I was a better football player. Beating him out would have provoked a serious if subtle crisis in the way the team operated.

In 1966 we played the Rams in an exhibition game in Los Angeles. We arrived a day early and Rick Sortun, Dave O'Brien, Chuck Logan and I rented a car and drove down to Hermosa Beach. We began fantasizing about how nice it would be not to have to go back to training camp and about having a beach house. Coming from an uptight masculine environment, we were about done in by the sight of bikini-clad women on the beach. We kept the car, and the next day, the day of the game, drove back down to the beach and stayed until about 3:30.

The Cardinals played a disastrously flat game against Los Angeles. We were already getting the hell beat out of us by half time, especially on defense, and Drulis began to chew us out. He said he was going to tell Winner to make us stay in the hotel instead of giving us the night off without curfew. We eventually lost 32 to 14, and true to his word, Drulis got Winner to announce that after we returned to the hotel we would have half an hour to get a sandwich and something to drink before we had to be in our rooms. Anybody who was not in at bedcheck faced a $1000 fine.

My roommate at that time, Dave Simmons, had been married shortly before training camp and had not seen his wife for about seven weeks. She had come out to visit a friend in L.A. and, thinking Dave would have the night off after the game, had registered at our hotel. She'd even managed to get the room directly across the hall from Dave's and mine. On the trip back to the hotel, Dave was crestfallen. There was his wife, within 30 feet, and he couldn't leave the room. Everyone else was mad too, if with less reason—some of the guys were so pissed off they kept throwing ashtrays and Gideon Bibles down on the sidewalk below their rooms. Until about two-thirty in the morning, Dave kept asking if I thought the coaches would come. I kept assuring him I would cover for him if they did and he finally mustered up enough nerve to cross the hall to see his bride. At six in the morning I heard a light rapping on the door. It was Simmons wanting to come in. I told him no coaches would be checking in the morning and to go back to his wife until our bus left for the airport around nine o'clock. He gratefully thanked me and left.

The third exhibition game was against Charley Winner's old team, the Baltimore Colts. I was assigned to the kickoff return team and my job was to block Lou Michaels, the Colts' kickoff man. Winner suggested that instead of running up and throwing a cross body block at Michaels, I should run up, stand in front of him and put my arms up like I was pass blocking him. He promised Michaels would stop dead in his tracks. I couldn't believe it, but I thought, "Well, hell he's the coach." Michaels kicked off. I ran up in front of him and just stood there, putting my arms up as if to pass block him. He was so flustered he stopped dead in his tracks for about five seconds, then tried to scramble around me. But his teammates were 30 yards down the field in front of him. The second time he kicked off I did the same thing and Michaels stopped again. It was really beautiful. I was keeping him completely out of the play and because he was caught so far upfield there was a natural hole right up the middle for our ball carrier. The third time I did this Michaels was really pissed off and he unloaded a left hook at my head, screaming as his fist bounced off my helmet.

On the next kickoff (Baltimore had many that night because they beat us 33 to 7) Michaels was anticipating my move. I could see him slowing up and pulling back his left fist, so instead of stopping as I had done before, I threw on the afterburner and whipped into him with a crossbody. He was slightly off balance when I hit him and went down like a weed. I quickly rolled away from him because I could hear him fuming and swearing "mother-fucking rookie." I jumped up, turned and laughed at him, and jogged off the field.

Because Bill Koman had beaten me out for the starting right linebacker position, I found myself on the bomb squads again. On the opening kickoff of the first game of the season, I was flying down the field gearing myself to take on the wedge which included one of the biggest football players I had ever seen, Philadelphia's offensive tackle, Bob Brown. I was going at Brown full speed, and the ball carrier was running about four yards behind him. I had two choices: either to bury myself into Brown, trying to make the runner stutter step so the other guys could make the tackle, or to fake Brown to my right and dodge him to my left, hoping to get by and make the tackle myself. I gave Brown a good fake, but as I was planting my right foot to move to my left, he threw out a huge forearm and caught me on the side of the helmet. I went down like a shot, intense pain shooting through my neck and shoulder.

I was writhing around on the field and the Cardinals called a time out. Jack Rockwell, the Cardinal trainer, came running out on the field to see what was the matter. They'd seen how hard I was hit and thought I had a broken neck. After I lay on the ground for a while, the pain began to subside and I was able to get up and walk off the field under my own power. The next week I went to a neurologist and he explained that Brown had hit me so hard on the head he had stretched all the nerves that ran along the right side of my spinal column. This was the hardest single blow I received in my 14 years of playing football.

19

As the 1966 season progressed, I began to play a fair amount, mainly on second and third downs when the coaches saw a sure passing situation. They knew I could cover halfbacks flaring out of the backfield and play pass defense much better than Bill Koman could because of my speed. During the season I played about 40 per cent of the defensive plays for the Cardinals.

When the season was over I returned to my graduate studies at Washington University, switching to the Department of Sociology. I continued my political work and became increasingly involved in the anti-war movement. In April of 1967, I attended the big peace march in New York with over 300,000 other people. A few weeks after I returned, I received a post card from Rick Sortun, saying he had driven down from Seattle to San Francisco to attend the companion peace rally held in Kezar Stadium.

About this time a good friend of mine, a student, stopped by our house on his way to his home in New York City and proceeded to introduce me to the business of smoking marijuana. I thoroughly enjoyed it. Later that spring my brother Dennis came out from Ohio. He was deep into psychedelics and brought an ample supply with him. One beautiful spring evening in St. Louis, I dropped my first tab of acid. It was exhilarating. Dennis stayed with me for about a week, and we dropped acid a couple of more times. During that same week, I gave a couple of Falstaff speeches. The contradiction between where my head was at while I was experimenting with acid and the location of the collective head of one of the St. Louis neighborhood Lion's Clubs was a real mindblower.

Although I was becoming more conscious politically, I hadn't yet fully understood football as a political phenomenon, or the way it resembled a circus for the increasingly chaotic American empire. But I was feeling my way in that direction. Dr. Horowitz, my advisor at Washington U., was helping me to rewrite my senior thesis on football because he felt it could be suitable for publication in *Trans-Action*. Meanwhile, Jim Gillespie, a friend who was studying at Southern Illinois University in Edwardsville, Illinois, invited me to speak about the war at two meetings he had set up with some fraternities and sororities on his campus. Southern Illinois is located in what might be called the heart of Middle America. Its students come from nearby small towns, and although the sons and daughters of this conservatism were stunned to hear a professional ballplayer criticize our involvement in Vietnam, they nevertheless listened to what I had to say.

About three weeks later, "Stormy" Bidwell, the Cardinals' president, called me and asked me to meet him at his office at the stadium concerning something he refused to discuss over the phone. When I went to see him, he said he'd received some letters from people around SIU at Edwardsville who were quite irate, and he wanted to know what anti-war groups I belonged to. I told him I'd appeared as a private citizen, not as a representative of the football Cardinals or of any specific political group. He was most concerned about my being a member of SDS. I told him that, although many of my friends in the movement were members of SDS, I was not. Stormy said he respected my right to protest the war but he warned me various groups would try to use my name because I was a professional player. We parted without animosity, although this was by no means the last I would hear of the matter.

Life as a football player makes one a victim of enforced schizophrenia. I was a football star half the year and another person for the rest, and I could not give myself completely to either identity. After my sophomore year at Syracuse, I'd quickly recognized that in order to grow emotionally and intellectually, I would have to divorce myself as much as possible from the "football mentality." I realized that spending time on the football field earned me a scholarship, and that this scholarship had to be the most important thing to me during my years at Syracuse. This is not to say I was immune to the football ethic; on the contrary, football gave me my identity, such as it was. Before I could quit playing football I had to learn what it was to be an individual. This won't seem very momentous to people who have grown up outside the world of athletics. But for a jock, becoming somebody real, getting involved in life off the playing field, is a significant problem. I imagine that in some small way it resembles what a priest who has always lived in a cloister must feel after he goes out, gets married, and tries to go on from there.

Early in July, 1967, Stacy and I bought an old funky townhouse in St. Louis. My two younger brothers, Dennis and Joe, came to help us move, and when we were done, Dennis informed me he had some acid. He and Stacy had decided to take some and he asked if I would too. I thought about it for five minutes, but finally declined. Making the down payment on the house had left us almost broke, and I had to make the football team in order to make myself solvent. Training camp was only about a week away, and I felt that taking the acid might diminish the football psych I'd been working to get up since the middle of May.

Because the Cardinals led the league in defense in 1966 and because I'd played well at linebacker, I received a $21,000 contract for 1967. Larry Stallings, our regular left linebacker, had been called into the Army to fulfill his ROTC commitment, and I expected to play regularly. But other things were on my mind. I felt guilty about spending my time playing football, and for the first time, I was not mentally prepared for training camp. I was losing the will to hit and this distressed me. In some ways I thought of myself—to quote Dylan—as "a pawn in their game." Yet, despite my strong feeling that I should step up my political activities and move farther away from football, the game was my only source of income. There was another complication: if I completed the '67 season, I would become a five-year man entitled to the benefits of the pension plan available to all vested NFL players.

I was in my uniform on the way to the practice field,

getting my psych together for the first major scrimmage in training camp, when an assistant trainer ran up and told me I had an emergency telephone call. I sprinted to the Cardinal training camp office in the players' dormitory. They had a secretary there and a separate room for Billy Bidwell, along with a teletype printing machine printing out the cut lists and trade information from the league office. As I ran, all sorts of possibilities flashed through my mind about something serious having happened to one of the children or to Stacy. Instead, it was a message from my brother Roger saying my younger brother Dennis had been busted the night before and put on $8,000 bail. He wanted to know if I could raise $800 to pay a bondsman to get him out. Charlie Shea, the Cardinals' treasurer, was in the office and I explained my predicament. I asked him for an advance on my salary and to have his secretary get me on a plane for Cleveland that night. Back at the practice field I had a horrible time in the scrimmage, and ended up terribly depressed about my play and about my brother.

20

In 1967, the racial tension that I'd seen simmering for years on the Cardinals finally reached the boiling point. What I saw around the locker room make me expect a race war at any moment.

I was first introduced to racism on the team, as I've said, in my rookie year, 1962; room assignments, wings of the dormitory, and the dining hall were all segregated. In the half hour between the end of practice and dinner, all the white ball players would head up to the town's only bar, the Lantern. I never saw a black football player in the Lantern at any time during my first five years with the team. The Cardinals had a strong southern clique, out and out rednecks who were the team leaders, including such guys as Sonny Randle, Bill Koman, Irv Goode, Joe Robb, Don Owens, and Ken Gray. Robb and Koman were the most vitriolic. Long before things came to the surface in 1967, Koman would continually tell me and anyone who'd listen that niggers were generally too dumb to play pro football, that pro clubs were giving niggers a break by having them around, etc.

Racism was not a matter of individual quirks in the St. Louis organization; it was part of the institution. For example, during my first six years with the Cardinals, the Falstaff Brewing Corporation gave parties for the players at Falstaff Inn. The Inn was two fairly large rooms separated by a large archway. One of the big surprises of my first year was the discovery that almost no blacks attended these parties, although Falstaff provided a free meal and all the beer you could drink after the games. When the blacks did begin to attend over the next few years, the squad usually broke up so the whites were in one room and the blacks in another.

Flying to the Dallas game in 1964, rookie Willis Crenshaw was sitting in the back of the plane with an empty seat next to him. Occasionally one of the stewardesses would sit down in the empty seat next to Willis. They talked casually throughout the flight. Sitting four rows in front of them were Joe Robb and Bill Koman. Koman began to turn around and stare at Willis, nudging Joe Robb to bring this "affair" to his attention. Our plane landed in Dallas and all the players and coaches were standing in a group in the Dallas Airport lobby waiting for the team buses. In front of the entire group, Robb singled out Willis and began chewing him out for trying to date white girls. I was standing halfway across the lobby, heard the noise and came over. "If I was you, I wouldn't try to make a white girl in front of the team. You are in Texas now," Robb was almost shouting. Robb berated him for a few more minutes and eventually walked away. Throughout Robb's tirade, Wally Lemm and his entire coaching staff did nothing.

Blacks who "knew their place" on the Cardinals were generally not harassed. This group was labeled "the decent niggers." Bill Koman told me that, "Prentice Gautt is the only really decent nigger on the Cardinals, and I might even have him out to my house for dinner." Even so, Koman, a church-going Catholic, couldn't accept the sincerity of Gautt's religious beliefs. Gautt, an active member of the Fellowship of Christian Athletes, was nicknamed "Elmer Gantry" by Koman.

Black ball players are selected even more stringently on the basis of "correct attitude" than whites. Blacks are in an especially difficult position; if they act like Toms, they will be completely dominated by the white ball players and lose respect for themselves and each other. But if they are too "militant" and try to assert their basic manhood by attempting to break out of the whites' stereotype of the shuffling, dumb, insensitive jock, they are immediately under suspicion and often cut from the squad.

Ed McQuarters, a defensive tackle from Oklahoma, was perhaps the best example of this dilemma. Ed was one of the quickest defensive linemen I have ever seen anywhere in football. But Charlie Winner said he felt McQuarters didn't have the correct attitude on the field. Actually, McQuarters' attitude was beautiful: he refused to take any shit from the whites. He carried himself with great dignity and certainly had the respect of his black teammates. Ed refused to smile at the cracks about black football players which were customary in training camp—white ball players talking about blacks' inherent ability to run fast or their congenital insensitivity to pain. In my opinion, and in the opinion of many other veterans, McQuarters would have been a great defensive tackle in the National Football League. But because he refused to demean himself, Winner cut him from the squad. When Ed was in camp, the coaches' complaints had nothing to do with his ability as a player, but with his aloofness and his inability to "laugh and joke along with the other players."

Another black, Bobby Williams, came to the Cardinals as an unsung college ball player. Bobby felt the quickest way he could make a name for himself was by playing cornerback and really tying into the team's prima donna receivers, most notably Sonny Randle, who happened to be a leader of the redneck clique. The first few days the veterans were in camp that year, Randle lost his helmet about three times: he'd casually catch a pass on a square-out pattern, and Bobby would come up and rap him good in the back of the head, knocking him out of bounds. As I said, there's an unwritten rule in camp against fighting with someone or yelling at him if he hits you hard—hitting is the name of the game—and all Sonny could do after he picked himself up off the ground was to glare at Williams. But Bobby Williams wasn't intimidated by the dirty looks, or by the snide comments: when Randle began taking his lumps regularly, Sonny's friends would always be hollering "Hey there, Cassius, how ya doin'?" at Bobby and asking him about Cassius Clay, who had changed his name to Muhammad Ali. Williams just kept hitting the veterans regularly and hard. He knew the only way he was going to make the Cardinals was to prove himself an out and out hitter.

One night in the spring of 1967, I arrived home after making a Falstaff speech and Stacy told me a guy by the name of Jack Olsen from *Sports Illustrated* had called and wanted me to return his call as soon as I could. I returned his call at his hotel in downtown St. Louis, and he asked if I could talk to him that evening.

I met Olsen around 10 o'clock that night. He was then doing research for his five part series on the black athlete and wanted to interview various Cardinal players about the racial situation which had flared briefly into the press at the close of the previous season. We established rapport immediately. Within five minutes, he was telling me about a phone conversation with Bill Koman. He said Koman was one of the worst racists he had ever talked to. "You wouldn't believe what that guy told me," he said. "I was down at El Paso, Texas, and the coaches and the townspeople down there were not as bad as Koman." We sat down with Olsen's tape recorder and rapped about the racial situation on the Cardinals for over two hours. I told him about the unconscious racism of the coaches and about the practice throughout the NFL of letting blacks play only in certain positions. (Very few blacks hold positions which are popularly thought to require a great deal of intelligence rather than a great deal of strength—such as linebacker, offensive guard and quarterback.) In our talk, I helped Olsen develop his thesis about the prevalence of stacking and racism throughout the National Football League. I was pleased to see that much of the information used in the last two parts of Olsen's series came from the football file I had accumulated since my senior year at Syracuse.

In my rookie year, Bill Koman had begun to buddy up and try to take me under his wing, as he did with a number of rookies he feared might eventually take his job. He would tell me that Chuck Drulis really had his eye on me, or that the coaches really thought I was going to be a good linebacker, or that Drulis had talked to him that afternoon and told him I should make the ball club easily. Since I thought Koman had a lot of pull, I wasn't about to disagree with him on any subject, and when he launched into one of his racist diatribes, I didn't confront him. But it wouldn't have mattered if I had; it was the management and coaching staff that gave segregation and racism their sanction and blessing. After all, it was the Cardinal staff that segregated the room assignments on the road; it was the Cardinal management that segregated the players into almost separate wings in the dormitories. And it was the Cardinal management that saw the growing gap between the white and black ball players and made no attempt to bridge it. The same thing is true at even higher levels. Pete Rozelle would hire detectives to spy on ball players during the season, but he never saw fit to police the racism and exploitation blacks faced. He never hired psychologists, say, to examine ways in which black and white ball players could associate more humanely, although individual clubs, the Cardinals included, would hire psychologists to aid them in selecting personnel and measuring a ball player's aggressiveness.

Near the end of the 1967 season, these tensions had become so intense that there was almost no communication between black and white ball players. It was a miracle we weren't forced to field two separate teams. The black players met secretly and drew up a list of grievances that had their unanimous support. These were presented to Charley Winner at the end of the season, and the next spring he called a meeting of all the players in St. Louis to discuss the racial situation. I was afraid Winner only wanted information about various players' attitudes, so I declined to go. I had been through these phony soul-searching sessions, and I knew that when the coaches were there, very little ever got said because each man feared that a misplaced phrase might mean disfavor.

News of this action by the Cardinals' blacks appeared—very briefly—in the St. Louis papers. The club made no formal statement, but the rumors were rampant, mainly that the blacks had pointed to a certain racist coach. After that season, three assistant coaches left the football Cardinals one by one, and each time rumors flew that this was the racist coach. Jack Olsen's article, however, revealed that the man the black players had in mind was Chuck Drulis. Even so, Head Coach Winner—the only coach with the authority to correct the situation—did nothing until the racism on the Cardinals was revealed publicly.

Even though being a black in the NFL—as in American society as a whole—is a devastating experience, I often felt that the blacks on the Cardinals team didn't take advantage of the momentum of the black revolution and certainly didn't help it. This is hard to understand, especially considering their own experience. Indeed, black professional football players have been glaringly absent from the struggles of black athletes on college campuses. To my knowledge, for instance, no black ball players registered any protest when Lloyd Eaton, coach at the University of Wyoming, kicked over a dozen black football players off his squad for wanting to talk about wearing black armbands in the game against racist Brigham Young University. Of course, black players are clearly in a bind. Stacking and quota systems do exist in the National Football League, and blacks who make it have more to lose than white ball players.

When I'd try to talk with the Cardinals' black players about the revolt of black college athletes, I'd usually get stony silence. Even so, on bus or airplane trips when I was reading *Ramparts* magazine and other publications, some of the blacks would come over and casually nudge me and ask if they could look at it. I'd give them the magazine, they'd leaf through it, then ask to borrow it for a few hours. I found myself constantly bringing the Black Panther newspaper with me to practice in the 1969 season and putting it in the black ball players' lockers. When they arrived for practice, they would glance over at me and kind of nod, but I was never able to engage them in a dialogue about what was happening to blacks in America, though there would be a spark every now and then. One particular time, John Roland came up to me and said he'd bought Eldridge Cleaver's speech at Syracuse University on an LP record. He was excited—"You should hear Eldridge run it down," he said. "He called this guy a racist motherfucking dog," and so on. This conversation was out of earshot of any coaches or other white ball players, of course, and nothing more came of it.

During my last few seasons, a few black ball players

got together for what they call "sets." This consisted of a mass sex scene at one of the player's apartments with several prostitutes, beginning immediately after practice and extending well into the night. These scenes were not unlike those organized by a prominent white player each year after the Cardinals broke training camp following the Chicago Bears game. He too would hire prostitutes and invite Cardinal ball players to "work out" in front of certain of his business associates in St. Louis who were excited by the spectacle.

Even in its orgies, the Cardinals team was Jim Crow all the way.

21

ASIDE FROM THE fact that all hell was breaking out between the blacks and whites on the team, 1967 was my worst year in pro football. I would practice all week with the first team defense, then bow out to Larry Stallings when he came back on weekends from Army duty to play the games. I began to question my abilities and to speculate about why, after five years in the league, I was still running insanely downfield under kickoffs on the bomb squad.

If I was less and less sure of the value of continuing to play pro ball, I was more and more involved with the antiwar movement. Late in September, Terry Koch, one of the leaders of SDS at Washington University, Marty Lebowitz, a graduate student in sociology, and I formed the St. Louis Mobilization Committee to organize and finance sending buses from St. Louis for the October 21 march on the Pentagon. I was sort of the treasurer—opening an account in the committee's name and signing all the expense checks. We managed to fill three large Trailways buses and four cars with marchers. I was only mildly surprised when, at the loading of the buses in a church parking lot near Washington University, two plainclothes St. Louis cops walked up to me and said, "Hi, Dave, how are things going?"

On the team's flight to Washington to play the Redskins later that season, Pat Fisher, who was sitting across the aisle from me, leaned over and said sarcastically, "Hey, what's this anti-war activity you've been doing?" I knew Pat was a conservative, and asked him what he meant. He said, "You know, sending those buses to Washington." I kind of smiled at him and said, "How did you know about that?" He motioned me over to an empty seat next to him and became serious. He whispered, "Didn't you know the FBI had you watched?" I asked him how the hell he knew that, and he said a friend of his had invited him to a party at the house of another friend who was an FBI agent. They discussed the recent activities at the Pentagon and the FBI agent told Pat, "Hey, do you know that one of your Cardinal teammates is a left-winger and into the peace movement in St. Louis? We have an extensive dossier on him, and we've been keeping him under surveillance." When Pat told me this, a chill went down my spine.

On December 7, three movement people were arrested for demonstrating in front of the Chase Park Plaza Hotel where Hubert Humphrey was giving an address. That evening, about 50 of us went down to the St. Louis Central Police Station to help arrange bail for these three.

We had been in the station for about half an hour, and I could see all the cops were getting uptight, when, suddenly, a high-ranking officer ordered the building cleared. About ten people sat down, and the rest left. Because Stacy and I were talking to a plainclothes cop who was taking graduate sociology courses at Washington University, we were not arrested. Those arrested were dragged off to the holding cell. One guy by the name of Paul Taxman was trying to leave, but was jumped by about ten cops who severely beat him with their night sticks. Later that night, Paul was finally taken to City Hospital with his face so badly smashed that the St. Louis Post-Dispatch—which normally approves all police activity—wrote an editorial entitled, "Thugs in Blue Uniforms." After the season, I organized the "Committee to Insure Constitutional Rights" to raise money for Paul. The police had not only broken Paul's face badly, but also damaged his vision in one eye. The corrective operation was to cost Paul $800 and we raised that much and more for him.

Then, in late December, Stacy received a call from Dale Drulis, Chuck's wife. During our first year in St. Louis, Stacy had worked for Dale, who is an artist and interior designer. That night she visited our home under a cloak of almost spy ring secrecy. When she left at 11:30, I sprinted up the stairs to my office and typed out this report of the conversation: "Dale Drulis, wife of Chuck Drulis, the St. Louis Cardinals' defensive coach, called and questioned my wife Stacy as to whether I intended to play football the following season (1968). She stated the reason for her questions was that she had some important information concerning my future in professional football with the St. Louis Cardinals and would stop by that evening to talk to me about this information.

"She arrived that evening and told me the reason for her visit and concern. The substance of her conversation is as follows: I would be contacted by Chuck Drulis acting as agent for the Bidwells to talk about my political activities, namely my organization and raising of money to send three buses from St. Louis to Washington for the protest march on October 21, 1967 at the Pentagon.

"She indicated that the FBI had contacted the Cardinal management with information that I had financed the trip and because of this they were concerned about my political involvement.

"Chuck Drulis was to inform me that I would not be allowed to pursue my various political activities if I intended to play football for the Cardinals next season. In short, I would be offered a choice. She said that Chuck was aware of her visit and had entrusted her to inform me of the impending conversation with him. She said both wanted me informed, giving me time to consider the alternatives I would be offered before I made my decision.

"The Bidwells were not aware of her involvement and she asked that I not contact them before Chuck had talked to me.

"She further stated that the FBI had me under surveillance and my phone was probably tapped, therefore I should be discreet in my future activities."

I was worried about what Dale had said and prepared to fight the Cardinals' management, so I composed a letter which I planned to make public if they pushed me. In mid-January I arranged to meet with Chuck Drulis at his house.

When he heard why I wanted to see him, he suggested we not meet at the Cardinal offices. I drove out to Chuck's home about nine in the evening and we began to talk. I could see he was uncomfortable. I began to reiterate his wife's conversation with me. To my great surprise he flatly denied much of what she had told me. "What about the FBI having me under surveillance and the FBI giving information to the Cardinal management?" I asked him. He shook his head and said he knew nothing of the FBI but that "certain Naval Intelligence people" had been snooping around the locker room and had been asking about my association with the football Cardinals. I could not understand his attitude. After he had repeatedly refused to tell me anything about the Cardinal management's decision to confront me about my political organizing, we began talking about the black players' list of grievances. He assured me that many of the players who had been most outspoken in their meeting with Charley Winner were second-stringers who were just hanging on the squad. But he admitted that Bill Koman, the leader of the racist clique, had been asked to retire by the Cardinal management.

Initially, I was perplexed by the two inconsistent stories. But after some investigative work of my own, it became clear why the Cardinals chose not to force the issue of my political activity at that time. The exposé of the racist situation on the Cardinals was imminent, and when they learned I planned to fight their attempt to gag me, they decided to back off, feeling the team could not afford two scandals in a single year.

22

ABOUT TWO WEEKS before the end of the '67 season, Bernie Parrish had asked Jim Bakken, our player representative in the National Football League Players' Association, to call a meeting at one of the motels in St. Louis. That night Parrish and Harold Gibbons, vice-president of the International Brotherhood of Teamsters, gave a presentation favoring a union—the American Federation of Professional Athletes—that Bernie was attempting to form with the Teamsters.

Bernie Parrish began pro ball with the Cleveland Browns in 1959 and had been nominated as an all-pro and played in the Pro Bowl game. After seven years, he wanted to leave the Browns. He asked to be released outright, rather than being put on waivers, because he knew Atlanta, starting its first year in the league, would pick him up. Parrish felt he had contributed much to the Browns' success and wanted to play for another NFL team other than the Falcons, but prior to the opening game of the 1966 season, Bernie Parrish was waived out of the league. It was unusual, to say the least, that not one club was interested in an all-pro defensive back at the peak of his career with seven years experience.

As an officer in the Players' Association, Bernie had begun to look into the financial condition of the National Football League. After 13 months of research, he had come up with some startling facts showing that the athletes were incredibly exploited. He decided the first step was to get rid of the fiction that the Players' Association—a sort of company union—had any leverage, and he approached AFTRA and the Screen Actors Guild before finally contacting Harold Gibbons of the Teamsters. Parrish and Gibbons then entered into an agreement to begin organizing all professional athletes in one pro players' union. Parrish's first concern was football players, but because he didn't want to be accused of upsetting players at the start of the season, he waited until mid-season to begin contacting clubs, and even then chose only those teams with absolutely no possibility of winning the championship.

When Parrish and Gibbons met with members of the Cardinals, they brought out some rather startling facts. Perhaps the most amazing statistic was this: during the period 1956-1967, the profits of the National Football League owners had increased 4300 per cent but the player salaries had gone up only 73.6 per cent. If you subtract rises in the cost of living during those years, our actual salary increases amounted to only 48.4 percent.

Gibbons outlined the relationship between the Teamsters and the new Association, and he emphasized that the players would not be tied directly to the Teamsters. At the close of the meeting, he passed out authorization cards and applications for membership in the American Federation of Professional Athletes. About 15 of the 20 guys there signed the cards. By the end of the season Parrish had seen all but five clubs in the National Football League and had authorization cards from more than 30 per cent of the players in the league.

At the annual Players' Association meeting, held during the first week of January 1968 in Miami (before the Runner-Up bowl game between Los Angeles and Cleveland), it was clear there was going to be a tremendous fight between certain interests in the Players' Association and the Parrish-Gibbons team. The issue was simply whether the Players' Association could conceptualize itself as a union and enter into collective bargaining with the league, or whether it was merely an association, as Norm Van Brocklin put it, to "enhance communication between the players and the owners."

Gibbons and Parrish had a debate with Clayton Miller, the Players' Association attorney, in the presence of the Los Angeles Rams and many of the player representatives from other NFL clubs. Miller was eventually so embarrassed in the confrontation that he got up and walked out in the middle of the meeting. The LA players were shocked and many were hollering at him, "Wait a minute, you can't walk out, you're our attorney." The following day a majority of the players' representatives who had seen this asked Miller to resign, which he did. That same day, Dan Schulman, a good friend of Players' Association President Mike Pyle, was hired as the new attorney.

Later that afternoon, the owners recognized the National Football League Players' Association as collective bargaining agents for the players in the NFL. Because of Parrish, the Players' Association was forced to take a militant stand. And the owners, fearing that the players would vote to affiliate with the Teamsters, agreed to bargain for the first time. It was the pressure that Parrish and Gibbons generated that forced the owners into collective bargaining with the Players' Association. Up until this time, the owners had adamantly stated that they would never enter into collective bargaining negotiations with the players.

Those players who opposed the Gibbons-Parrish unionization plan based their argument on the claim that they were not workers. Players like Jim Bakken felt that we should conceive of ourselves as professionals, and that it would have been degrading to be unionized. It's strange: pro ball players will allow coaches to totally dominate their lives even to the extent of telling them when they have to go to sleep, but they still claim to be professionals. The workers that ball players look down their noses at don't take that kind of shit from the bosses. For that matter, even college co-eds have organized and rebelled against bedtime restrictions.

The Players' Association has no real power comparable to what the players in the league could have had if they had accepted affiliation with the Teamsters. The Players' Association has yet to win pro ball players any real say in their working conditions. While it is true that many ball players get paid good salaries, they have as much say over their actual working conditions as the workers in one of Andrew Carnegie's steel mills had in the 19th century.

It was good to see John Mackey's outspoken leadership during the 1970 players' strike, but it's depressing
that the players' primary concern was just for money.
While it is true the players are being ripped off compared
to the enormous profits most owners are making, in reality
the ball players are being paid pretty damn well for six
months work. What is wrong with professional football is
not that the players are not getting a decent wage, but the
dehumanizing conditions they are required to work under.
Players are naive to expect sportswriters or the public to
support their demands for more money; however, there
are many who could actively support them if they strug-
gled to be treated as grown men. What is needed is a
strong union, for it is obvious that the Players' Association—even after its hollow 1970 contract "victory"—does
not have sufficient strength or political savvy to challenge
the owners' total control over the players' lives and identity. Every player is aware of the racism that exists
throughout the league, yet the Players' Association never
forces the owners to correct this situation, or at least honestly admit that it exists. The Association was heading in
the right direction, however, when it identified and challenged Rozelle as the owners' agent. When Rozelle regularly involves himself in scrutinizing players' off-the-field
activities but fails regularly to do the same for the owners,
there should be no question about who owns him. If any
more proof is needed, it should be recognized that the
owners, not the players, can have him fired.

No matter how much ball players like to picture themselves as professionals, they are still workers who can be
fired, traded, or black-balled out of professional football

at the whim of an owner; workers who make good money but are subjected to incredible psychological conditions. In their desire for greater profits, owners will do whatever is necessary, regardless of the effect it may have on individual ball players. Perhaps some day professional ball players will realize that there could quite easily be professional football without owners, who are the only irrelevant party to the sport. It was amazing to me that during the 1970 Players' Association strike, no one suggested the Players' Association conduct the regular season games itself. The Association could have negotiated a TV contract, rented stadiums and played the games. Among other things, cutting out the owners' tremendous profits would allow the players to still get adequate salaries, while at the same time allowing for a drastic reduction in the price the fans must pay for tickets.

23

IN THE SPRING OF '68 I returned to my graduate studies at Washington University. I was still working on my study of football, but my community organizing had increased so much I was spending almost all my time working in the movement in St. Louis. In April '68 the local SDS held a regional meeting. After gathering initially on the campus, the meeting adjourned to my house for discussion groups. There were probably about 150 people milling around inside, in the front of, in the back of, and on the side of my house. The neighbors seeing all the wild-looking longhairs were really getting uptight. At one point, I went upstairs in search of my daughter Jennifer, thinking she was in my son Chris' bedroom. When I turned the knob and tried to go into the room, I met surprisingly strong resistance. I managed to open the door a crack and poke my head in and there, under clouds of blue cigarette smoke, sat about 25 women in heated discussion. The talk stopped and all eyes focused on me. I was informed that this was a caucus of Women's Liberation and that I could go now.

The JOIN Community Union people from Chicago had also come down for the conference, including Mike James, who is now organizing young working class guys in Chicago. Mike and I hit it off immediately. He had been a football player at Lake Forest College, and had then gone out to Berkeley on a Woodrow Wilson fellowship and had become radicalized. We spent some time together exchanging views.

I had been going through some changes—feeling extremely guilty about my $25,000 house, worrying that I was contributing too little to the movement and thinking that my life had little meaning. I was getting ready to make a major decision about football when, in February 1968, my third child, Sarah, was born. She was a severe microcephalic—a condition which will require custodial care all her life. Placing her in a private home cost over $3500 a year and so I felt more trapped than ever and with no chance of resolving the contradiction in my life. I needed money but had no prospects other than football. I resigned myself to going back again.

That spring my house was constantly filled with movement people. It was large and comfortable, and an ideal central meeting place. But Stacy, who was under great emotional strain because of Sarah, soon had to field 25 calls a day and I began to feel that old need to isolate myself from a reality that greatly threatened my desire to play football. So, on May 1st, I decided to drop out: I changed my phone number, stopped going to meetings and stopped having them at my home. I lived as a recluse trying to get my football psych back, going outdoors only to work out.

There was one exception: Bill Briggs, a defensive end for the Washington Redskins whom I got to know during the winter of '68, was actively involved in the McCarthy campaign. We had discussed the merits of McCarthy and Kennedy that winter, and I'd explained to Bill that I couldn't see actively supporting either man. But early that summer, the McCarthy people put on a party in New York City to woo supporters from the now leaderless Kennedy campaign, and when Briggs called from Washington to invite me, I accepted.

The party was held half a block from Central Park, and many of the big McCarthy supporters were there—Arthur Miller, Allard Lowenstein, Leonard Bernstein, Dwight MacDonald and others. It was all a sort of grotesque liberal trip and it was a little nauseating. The elitism of the McCarthy people could not be ignored. I remember wondering where the poor people were, or the blacks. Then I did see two black people: they were serving drinks and food.

I went to training camp in 1968 without having agreed on a contract. This was also the first year I went in with the veterans instead of going in early with the rookies. The linebacker coach, Don Shroyer, had a meeting the evening we arrived in training camp following Charley Winner's general meeting. I waited around until all the guys had left and asked Don point blank what the Cardinals planned for me. He informed me that he wasn't sure where I fit in with the Cardinals' plans. I was stunned and outraged. I immediately went up to Coach Winner's office. He could see I was really pissed and admitted I'd be fighting it out with three other guys for the swing spot behind

Stallings and Ernie Clark, who had come to the Cards in exchange for Joe Robb. I left the meeting in almost tearful rage. I couldn't believe the Cardinals had done this to me. I had played for five years behind Koman and done a credible job. When he retired, I expected at least to be given the opportunity to handle the starting position.

Coming off a fairly hectic off-season of political organizing combined with Sarah's birth and the business of facing the ugly reality that football was now inextricably a part of my life, Winner's news really blew my mind. Everything seemed to be going against me, and I felt the Cardinals were only keeping me around because they needed an experienced back-up man for Larry Stallings, whose Army obligation wasn't over. My response was to stop worrying about whether or not I was going to make it. I reckoned that one of my problems in earlier years was continually worrying about gaining the coaches' approval. And for the first time I just went out and worked--with my usual fanaticism but without thinking too much of how the coaches assessed my performance.

I was really at odds with my world, and the irony was that football gave my life structure. At times, I felt I was really flipping out, and that I'd be in the loony bin if it wasn't for the simple regularity of training camp. I could always depend on how practices would go and how stable the football routine was. It was the only time I was ever grateful for the game's authoritarianism.

Three days before the fifth part of Jack Olsen's "The Black Athlete: A Shameful Story" hit the newsstands, an advance copy was sent to the Cardinals because it dealt solely with the racism in their organization. At the eight o'clock meeting that evening, Charley Winner passed out Xerox copies of Olsen's piece, told us to read it and then be back in the meeting room by nine o'clock to discuss what it said. When I returned, I found the coaching staff, owners and the entire squad there. The Cardinal organization naively believed the players would let their hair down and openly discuss the contents of Olsen's article in front of the owners and coaches. The assumption was that we were one big happy family of professional football players and could freely discuss the exceedingly volatile contents of Olsen's article.

Winner's opening speech went something like this: "You know newspapers and magazines always need to find something, some bit of information that they can sensationalize." He said flatly that the problems pointed out in Olsen's piece did not exist and that *Sports Illustrated* had exaggerated a few minor points of normal player friction only to sell more copies. Mike Strofolino immediately got up and seconded Winner with a mealy-mouthed speech about how he had experience with the Baltimore Colts, the Rams and Cardinals, and our team had nothing more than normal tensions. At that point, Ernie McMillan, the Cardinals' veteran black tackle, stood up, threw down his notebook and screamed, "That's bullshit. It's all bullshit. Every word of that story in *Sports Illustrated* is true." He accused Winner and Strofolino of trying to play down real problems. He said, "I will personally stand on every word that's printed in that article." At this point Winner became almost paralyzed because honest emotion was threatening to get loose. He assured Ernie that he was not only aware of some of the problems but indeed had gone to great lengths to correct them and admonished him not to be so passionate. Winner kept insisting that we could handle these problems ourselves. He felt that after the black players had presented him with their list of grievances, he had done much to correct the racial attitudes of assistant coaches and the various players that were mentioned then Cid Edwards got up and said, "The real problem is how white football players feel blacks always want to jump in the rack with their wives and any white woman they see on the street. You white guys ask any of us here who we like, and I'm sure that, to a man, every black football player will say he prefers black women." He continued, "That's the reason why you guys get upset—because you think that we want to screw every white woman we see." The squirming throughout the room indicated that Edwards had indeed struck one of the sensitive nerves of white football players' racism.

Willis Crenshaw cited Olsen's article in mentioning our safety, Jerry Stovall, a Southern Baptist who held Bible meetings at the training camp. Stovall denied the racism Willis accused him of, closing his argument as follows, "Why, I even took Prentice Gautt [the Cardinals' black halfback] into my parish church in Monroe, Louisiana . . ."

Throughout the meeting, Winner was in a constant state of agitation. He kept coming down heavy on anybody who showed signs of real discontent and disagreement and after a while the players got fed up and realized no honest dialogue would take place in that meeting and any player who spoke the truth would surely face reprisals. Winner was trying to whitewash the whole problem. His closing line was that we must be a football team and that our prime concern was to go win a championship. He suggested we skip the regular football meeting that night and that all of us, black and white, should go down to the Lantern and have a few beers. At this point I almost fell out of my chair; Rick Sortun and I looked at each other incredulously. Winner hoped to solve a ten year problem of racist behavior among coaches and white ball players by having the guys go down to the Lantern, a place from which black players had been informally banned until recently, and drink a few beers together.

On the field, training camp was going very well for me. Yet when Larry Stallings came back from the Army for a week of practice, I was demoted to second team and resented the indignity of the move. All this time I was still haggling contract with the owners. I felt that if I continued to have good scrimmages I would be able to approach the salary that I wanted. After each scrimmage, I would go talk to Charlie Shea, the club treasurer, who was negotiating my contract. I kept doing well, and the amount he offered kept increasing. Finally, on the day of the first exhibition game in St. Louis, I signed for $24,000 base salary with a $6000 bonus clause. The bonus clause was broken up into four parts. If I played in 17½ per cent of the defense plays, I would receive $1500 and it would go up until I reached $6000 at 75 per cent of the scrimmage plays on defense.

I was completely satisfied with this contract and began playing half of each exhibition game. Larry Stallings was able to play in most of the exhibition games and rotated with me and Ernie Clark. We played Kansas City for the first time in Kansas City for the Governor's Cup, a newly created award for the champion professional football team of Missouri. Kansas City beat us but I had a great night. On one particular play, Mike Garrett attempted to run a pass pattern on me, but I wasn't faked into coming up for the run and chugged him as he got to the line of scrimmage. As he caught the ball, I tackled him for a two yard loss in the backfield. When we saw the films the following Monday, Dick Voris, our newly acquired defensive line coach, was ecstatic about my play. I still wasn't convinced that I'd won a starting berth but felt that I had made a great stride toward it. I also watched how Ernie and Larry did and I must admit I was pleased when they made mistakes and fucked up.

My contract made it financially important to me to play as many defensive plays as possible during the regular season. At the same time, the team, including myself, was attempting to win a division championship. So, where I was able to pick up a particular tip on the opposition, I was confronted with the dilemma of whether or not to share it with the other linebackers. Coaches constantly talk about team spirit but I've always wondered how the hell there can be team spirit if I know that the more other linebackers screw up, the more I'll be able to play, and the more I play, the more money I make. Owners keep writing contracts with performance clauses such as the one I had, though these can only work to create divisiveness on the team, for these clauses create a situation where the amount of money a player gets is dependent on how badly his teammates at his position play. A second string player who will not get his bonus unless he plays at least 40 per cent of the plays will not be upset if the guy ahead of him screws up badly. The owners introduced these bonuses with the idea that they would extract better performances from the players and result in more victories. In reality, just the opposite usually happens. Rumors began to spread around the league during the 1969 season that receivers who had bonus clauses for the number of passes they caught were paying kickbacks to the quarterbacks.

This dual level of competition is built into pro football. On one hand, the player is competing against his opponent, the guy across from him, and wants to do a good job to further the club's success. At the same time, I was constantly aware that my every move would be on movie film and would be scrutinized closely by the coaching staff the following Monday when they decided between me and my competitors on the team for the starting role. This competition involved not only linebackers, but also halfbacks that I had to cover in practice: if they looked good it meant that I wasn't doing my job and that could get me demoted to second team.

Players bullshit the press on how they help the various rookies. I have rarely seen this happen—certainly I received no help at all when I was a rookie. Quite the contrary, rookies generally received constant abuse from the vets, designed to intimidate them and break their confidence. The new player must not only prove himself on the field, he must also prove he can take their harassment. It's survival of the fittest from beginning to end.

24

SINCE THE CARDINAL training camp in Lake Forest is only 35 miles north of Chicago, I was aware of all the preparations Daley's cops were making to counter the people who were going to the Democratic Convention to protest against America. I was feeling somewhat cut off and isolated because I was stuck at a professional football training camp, and searching for some political contribution I could make. One night I asked Rick Sortun what he would think of us writing a petition supporting Eugene McCarthy and seeing how many ball players we could get to sign it. Rick said he felt McCarthy was merely a reformist who would never bring about the kind of significant changes the society needed, even if he were elected. He agreed, however, that the petition would be a good tactic to make the players aware of the coming confrontation between the forces of peace and forces of war at the Democratic Convention.

After our usual evening team meeting, Rick and I, together with Dave O'Brien and Chuck Logan, went out for a few beers. With some help from them, I wrote the petition, making it as mild as possible. "Because of the critical state of the Democratic Party and the nation, we professional football athletes feel compelled to announce our support of Senator Eugene J. McCarthy as the Democratic nominee for President of the United States. As professional football players and concerned young men, we have become aware of the need in this country for Senator McCarthy's positive and progressive policies concerning the Vietnam war and the urban crisis. It is our collective opinion that Senator McCarthy's position on the major issues facing this nation most represent the feelings of young people and progressive thinking adults in this country. If we are to salvage the concept and practice of the democratic process and also include the 'disaffected' generation of young people, Senator McCarthy's nomination is imperative. Therefore, as concerned young men and professional athletes, we support Senator McCarthy."

The next day I called Stormy Bidwell, President of the Cardinals, and read him the petition. He was sympathetic and gave his O.K. Then I took the petition around, expecting little support. But 17 guys signed it, including such name ball players as Charley Johnson, John Roland, Dave Williams, Bob Reynolds, Roy Shivers, and most surprising of all, Bobby Joe Conrad. Bobby Joe was from Texas A & M. He was an older veteran whom I knew very slightly. I'd assumed he was politically to the right, but when I solicited his name for the petition he said, "Sure, I'll sign it, is there any place where I can send money to support McCarthy?" I called Kitty Madeson, wife of McCarthy supporter Marvin Madeson, and read her a copy of the petition over the phone. Now head of the New Democartic Coalition, Madeson was one of the few Missouri delegates in the McCarthy camp. The next day he called a news conference outlining the strategy as he conceived it for the McCarthy people in Chicago. At the end of the news conference, he read the petition and distributed copies to the press.

Not one word about the petition ever appeared in the St. Louis newspapers, although the McCarthy headquarters put the petition in telegram form and sent copies to each of the Missouri delegates.

After we returned from our exhibition game against New York in New Haven, Connecticut, Rick, Dave O'Brien and I went down to the convention. We talked to many of the Missouri delegates but went away with nothing but a strong impression of their cynicism, insincerity, and old age. We finally ended up at a party at McCarthy headquarters while all hell was breaking loose outside. We couldn't afford to risk being arrested, but I knew, as Rick did, that our people were in the streets.

I had won a starting job at right linebacker. We lost our first game of the season to Los Angeles. The next game was played in San Francisco. Gary Lewis was in the 49er backfield with Ken Willard; together they were the biggest backfield we were to face all year. The former Cardinal halfback, John David Crow, was starting at tight end and Sonny Randle, another ex-Cardinal, was starting at split end for the 49ers. In the first quarter San Francisco had the ball on a third down with one yard to go. The 49ers ran a 37 slant—a play designed to go right over my position. I easily shed John David's block, slipped the pulling guard and hit Lewis with the front of my head, catching him about six inches above his knees. He went down like a bag of wet cowshit and didn't make the necessary yard. I went down on my hands and knees and "smelled the grass." (When I'd get hit really hard on the head, the grass would have a peculiarly pungent odor and I knew I'd been dinged pretty good when I smelled the grass that particular way.) I went over to the sideline and got an ampule of ammonia from the trainer and it seemed to clear my head.

That Sunday turned out to be a long day for the defense. We were in almost 80 plays and it was fairly hot in San Francisco. In the fourth quarter, Gary Lewis (who weighs about 230 pounds and has massive legs) ran a 37 flow to my side. As he started, he could see we had closed off all running room for him and reversed his field. I went after him, having eliminated in my mind all San Francisco players who could block me. I was closing in on Lewis going full speed when the 49er's Howard Mudd blindsided me. It was one of the hardest blocks I'd ever been hit with in professional football, and I literally went flying through the air, landing on the back of my head. I remember from watching the films and reflecting on the game that after I hit the ground I rose slightly, saw Lewis was going to be tackled, and lay back down on the field. I wasn't knocked out or dinged, just stunned by the impact of Mudd first hitting me and then me hitting the ground.

On our ride to the airport after the game, I began to feel nauseous, and when we arrived, I went behind the bus and threw up. I had the dry heaves. They first put me on the airplane, but then held up the plane and called an ambulance to rush me to St. Mary's hospital in San Francisco because the team physician thought I had a severe concussion. The dry heaves lasted a couple of hours; then I was finally able to sleep. The X-rays showed no broken bones in my head, and the next evening I flew back to St. Louis with Dr. Fred Reynolds, the team physician, who had stayed over to watch my progress.

On Tuesday, when watching the game films, I noticed the coaches were a little cool towards me, even though the films showed I had played an excellent football game. Dr. Reynolds told me I would be unable to play the following week against New Orleans. That week I didn't practice at all, although I did come to practice and attended the meetings. I missed the New Orleans game in which the Cardinals scored their first victory of the season. The headaches I'd been having subsided by Tuesday of the following week. I practiced all week and started the game against Dallas. I was nailed fairly hard a couple of times on my head, particularly when tackling Don Perkins, the toughest running back in the league since Jim Brown retired. I'd played a good ball game, but immediately after it was over I was wracked with severe headaches which continued until Friday of the next week. I went to visit Reynolds and he was clearly worried. I'm sure he felt I'd returned to duty too soon and that I might have aggravated the concussion I had incurred in San Francisco. He put me through a maze of exams and tests and found nothing. I remember that week as about the dingiest of my life: with the steady headaches and a hazy feeling of unreality, I had a difficult time remembering where I was or what I was doing.

The game after Dallas was against Cleveland. I stayed home and watched it on television. The week after the Dallas game was very strange. Although I was attending the meetings, the coaches refused to speak to me. Finally on Thursday, Drulis asked me how I was. Clearly, they were suspicious about my injury—because it wasn't evident, couldn't be put in a whirlpool or strapped with an analgesic pack. It had something to do with the head and the mind and football coaches are very suspicious about such things. They would be very happy if the mind could be as mechanical and predictable as a bicep. They thought of me as a little freaky anyhow and weren't sure that the dings I'd received in San Francisco and Dallas wouldn't render me too freaky to accept the routine of professional football. They evidently decided to leave things alone. After the Cleveland game, which the Cardinals won, I resumed my regular starting role and played great football throughout the remainder of the season.

That year we played Baltimore, and for the first time in my pro career I was able to go against John Mackey, my former teammate at Syracuse and now an all-pro tight end and the best blocking end in the National Football League. I'd been itching to play against him since we both entered the league in 1963, yet except for a few isolated exhibition games, we had not had a chance to square off. On one particular sequence of plays, Baltimore had the ball on our three yard line going in for a score. In watching game films all week, I'd learned that Baltimore's favorite goal line play was a 37 straight to take advantage of Mackey's tremendous blocking. This play went directly over me. Mackey came up and dropped into his stance; he tilted his weight a little bit forward and his forearm was shaking slightly. That was all the clue I needed, for I knew the play was coming right over me. I dropped into a slightly lower stance, and as soon as Mackey's head moved a fraction of an inch, I unloaded with my left forearm and caught him in the chest, picking him up off his feet and driving him two yards into the backfield. John grunted, "Good hit, man." On second down Baltimore ran a play in toward the center of the line and drove the ball to the one yard line. On third down I saw Mackey go into his stance again, arm trembling. This time I crouched a little lower because I knew I had surprised him the first time. My eyes were glued to his helmet because John, like many tight ends in the league, dips his head slightly before he charges at the snap of the ball. So, as soon as I saw the little nod, I unleashed my forearm and was able to get underneath John's block. I drove him back about a yard and the play was thrown for no gain. Finally, on the last down, Baltimore scored on a play pass to Tom Matte. When reviewing the films the following Tuesday, Dick Voris, who had been coaching in the western division and watching Mackey's play since he came into the league, said that was the best play he'd seen by any linebacker made against John. I was immensely pleased. I had gone against the very best and, in that sequence of plays, had been the victor.

In 1968 I played well because I needed to prove to myself more than anyone else that I could play in the

National Football League. After a shaky start, in which we lost three of our first four ball games, we went on to win all but one game the rest of the season, and that was against Baltimore which went on to win the NFL championship.

After the season, I picked up my $6000 bonus and reflected on my uncertainty of only a few months earlier. I had proven myself to the coaching staff and I knew that I had overcome my fears and anxieties about playing in the National Football League. Now it was time to move on to other things. To celebrate my success, Stacy and I took a two week vacation in the Virgin Islands. I still had no idea of what I was going to do, but was living in the glow of having had a good year. The one disturbing thing was my feeling that a good part of my life was still unfulfilled and that to continue playing football with the total dedication that I had shown in 1968 would be a great compromise.

The only thing I had going for me after my return from the Virgin Islands was being enrolled in graduate school at Washington University. I began my studies again, yet felt the university setting added less and less meaning to my life. Though I'd done a lot of thinking about who I was, I never seemed able to know my real feelings about many things. There was, in short, much ambivalence in my life. Then, in the last week of March '69 I attended a five day workshop at Esalen Institute led by Seymour Carter. My experience at Esalen was, to make an understatement, significant. I saw very acutely the contradiction between the feelings I had during my experiences at Esalen and the experiences I had working within my craft, which was football. Since high school, I had

been using the mask of "football player" to confront the
world. It was both my main line of defense and my main
source of gaining approval and recognition. I also realized,
paradoxically, how cut off and removed I was from my
body. I knew my body more thoroughly than most men
are ever able to, but I had used it and thought of it as a
machine, a thing that had to be well-oiled, well-fed, and
well-taken-care of, to do a specific job. My five days at
Esalen left me with an immensely good feeling. I had
glimpsed a bit of myself and realized that the "me" behind the face guard was alive and well and could feel and
think.

I felt more than ever that my role as football player
was a sham. It kept me from responding and communicat-
ing on a human level with other people. Esalen was a
benchmark and in many ways a beginning for me.

Sam Dardick, president of DGH & Associates, a St.
Louis city-planning firm, had a contract to do advocate
planning for the Kansas City Model Cities proposal. Sam
hired me as a consultant. We had an office in a ghetto of
Kansas City and my special project was to develop—that is
articulate—the needs and desires of various young guys
who lived in the Model Cities target areas. The proposal
we wrote was accepted in total by the Model Cities director. When I returned from Kansas City, I went down to
the Cardinal offices in Busch stadium to pick up my shoes
and sweatpants to begin working out. I was sitting in the
office of Joe Pollack, the public relations director, when
Dick Voris, the defensive line coach, walked in. I looked
up and smiled, and said, "Hi, Coach, how's everything
doing?" He took one look at me and said, "When are you

going to get your hair cut?" My hair wasn't outrageously long but I'd let it become a little shaggy during the off-season. I was unable to respond to his question with the scorn it deserved and realized I wasn't completely free from worrying about the coaches' approval.

Late in the spring, when I went down to the stadium to pick up a new pair of football shoes, I ran into Voris again. This time he grabbed a hold of me and began shaking my hand. He pulled me close and I felt his left hand running over my body. I had two very strange feelings go through me while he was touching me and asking, "How's your weight, you workin' out, you gettin' in shape, you look a little thin." The first one was a repugnance at being handled like a piece of meat; the second was a warm feeling because he was expressing "fatherly" concern about me. It was a sort of psychological civil war.

As a way of trying to convince myself that I really wanted to play, I was getting myself in fantastic shape for the 1969 season. For the first time I arrived in training camp under 225 pounds, weighing 220. I had tried to put all my doubts about playing out of my mind and worked like a demon to get into great shape.

That spring, I got to know Chuck Drulis, Jr., the son of our head defensive coach. Chuck had been an outstanding end at Duke but got a serious shoulder injury and didn't make it in the pros. Chuck and his wife, Ripple, went with Stacy and me to some music scenes over at Southern Illinois University. Chuck had some Nepalese hash which really lifted my head up. I found that being in condition was really great for smoking dope—with my lungs in shape, I could inhale a tremendous volume of smoke. I also found I could go out the next day and run without experiencing any bad after-effects. I had smoked cigarettes on and off throughout college and in the pros and found they really cut down my wind, but smoking marijuana or hashish didn't affect me at all.

This year, the Cardinals only had seven linebackers in camp because Don Shroyer, the linebacker coach, said he knew who was going to play and didn't want a lot of dead weight around. I reported with the rookies as did Larry Stallings, Jamie Rivers, and Rocky Rosema. When I first saw Shroyer, he was mildly surprised, but said he was glad because it showed we were interested in dedicating ourselves to making a team of championship caliber. Shroyer said, "Dave, if you don't make All-Pro linebacker, I'm going to kick your butt."

There's nothing wrong with being an All-Pro, and I would have liked being named All-Pro during my career; but my feeling at the time was more one of measuring up to the coaches' expectations than of doing well for myself. More than in any of the preceding years, I felt great pressure to avoid thinking of my doubts about playing football. But no amount of effort could rid me of the knowledge about myself which had led me to understand that football was no longer necessary in my life.

Rick Sortun came in with the veterans, and I went over to his room before the six o'clock supper. We looked at each other almost as if to say, "What in God's name are you doing back here?" We shook hands and began to talk about what we'd done in the off-season. Finally, I turned to Rick and said, "What the hell are we doing here?" He said, "I don't know, but I'm pretty sure this is my last year." I said I'd done a lot of thinking and had pretty much decided the '69 season would be my last one too. We looked at each other and said, almost simultaneously, "Let's shake on that." So we made a pledge to each other, shook hands and walked over to the chow hall for supper.

25

AFTER THE VETERANS had been at training camp about three days Jack Rockwell began passing out psychological examinations without first consulting any of the players. Rockwell just assumed everybody would do as he was told. When he passed out the exams, I held up my hand and Jack came over. I asked him whether or not the exams were mandatory. He said, "Well, you're not required to take them but I don't see any objection." I asked him again very specifically if we had to take them and he said no. So Rick, who was sitting next to me, and I walked out. The next night at dinner, Rockwell came over and asked quite indignantly why I hadn't taken the exam. He had been talking to Stormy Bidwell, who was staring over at our table with an upset look on his face. I told Jack that I had proven myself in the league and didn't feel it was necessary for the Cardinals to have information about my attitudes. I also told him I objected to his failure to consult the players and ask their permission before passing out the exam. I can't forget Bob DeMarco's classic line after he had taken the test. He said, "Just think. I've been in the

league nine years and an All-Pro, now I find out I'm a
pussy." A pussy is a football word for a guy who's chickenshit.

Having Stacy and the kids at Lake Forest for the first
time was great. After supper, I used to drive over to the
house we'd rented and spend an hour and a half with the
kids, taking them for an ice cream cone or down to the
beach. I'd whip back to the eight o'clock meeting and
when it was over, drive back to the house and spend about
an hour with Stacy. It was a welcome reprieve from the
rigor of training camp. We had our little stash of grass, but
I was only smoking after the Saturday scrimmages the first
couple of weeks because we were in heavy double days.

We had our annual rookie show at training camp,
and it is a tradition that after the rookie show everybody
troops down to the Lantern in Lake Forest and gets roar-
ing drunk. Since I wasn't into boozing, I looked forward to
spending a couple of extra hours at home on the night of
the show. As the groups were breaking up and heading
toward their cars to drive to the Lantern, a black guy on
the team walked up and laid two joints on me. I smiled
and nodded my thanks. I didn't know him very well but
we had flashed on each other and figured that we were
like-minded about dope. I slipped the joints into my shirt
pocket and turned to go out with Rick. As I got to my car I
realized I wasn't sure if this guy ran with his black brothers or not. I'd assumed he would be going out and getting
boozed up with his black teammates, but I didn't know. I
was feeling really pretty bad about not asking him to join
me at my house to smoke the joints, so I turned around
and went back in. I found him and said, "I kind of apolo-

gize that I didn't ask you what you're doing tonight," and then asked him if he'd like to come over to my place, listen to some music and smoke the grass. He said sure. As we were driving to my house, I asked him whether he went out very much with his black teammates. He said no, that those guys are so straight they don't really know where it's at. So we stopped over at my place and had a very relaxing time.

This guy and I got to know each other during training camp and he told me he was expecting a "care package" from home. He went to get the stuff from the Lake Forest post office during the break one afternoon. He came into my room carrying a pretty good size brick and asked if he could stash it in my closet because his roommate was always snooping around and might find the stuff if he kept it in his room. I said sure, there was no sweat. So we put the key up in my suitcase and there it stayed for the remainder of training camp. Since he had a good supply we would regularly go over to my house after the evening meeting and toke up. It was like the scene in M.A.S.H. where the team is high on the bench.

The exhibition season went fairly well for me. I was playing as well as I had the previous year. In the fourth quarter of the Minnesota game in Memphis, Bill Brown, the Vikings' great fullback, ran a draw play. I had picked up my initial key telling me it was a pass and dropped out about four yards to cover when my second key told me it was a draw and I came flying up into the hole to meet Brown, who was carrying the ball. Brown is one of the most powerful fullbacks in the National Football League. I went into him low and caught his knee right square in the middle of my forehead. He hit me so hard I didn't even remember what happened. I was completely out of my mind for the rest of the first quarter though I played almost seven minutes more. As I saw later in the game films, I was playing completely by instinct. The only tipoff that something was wrong was when I covered a flood pattern: Jamie Rivers, our middle linebacker, and I had agreed before the game to switch assignments on that particular pass pattern but I handled it in the standard way.

At the end of the first quarter I went off the field, and Don Shroyer asked me why I didn't switch off on that particular coverage. I looked at him point blank and said, "What coverage?" Seeing the glazed look in my eye he asked, "How many defenses did we have?" and I said, "What defenses?" Then he asked, "Do you know you're playing a football game?" I said, "Yes, but what football game?" He said, "Listen, I think you've been hit on the head, and you'd better go sit down." I went over and sat on the bench. Jack Rockwell came over and cracked an ampule of ammonia and held it under my nose but all it did was make my eyes water. I remember very clearly sitting with my arms along the back of the bench, legs stretched out, relaxing, watching the action. It was like a surrealistic dream. All the players and the coaches were uptight because Minnesota was kicking the hell out of us. I was fully cognizant of the defenses and could almost see beyond them; I could see the dynamic of the football game precisely. It was very strange: though I was completely out of touch with that reality I could converse about the game, about the defenses at any time. Larry Stallings would regularly come over and we'd rap about what went down in the previous series. I was fairly lucid and offered suggestions as to how he might modify his play to handle certain Minnesota plays.

The next game was to be played against Kansas City in St. Louis and Charley Winner was determined to win the game and the Governor's Cup this time. Because of my injury, I just stood around and watched practice in a pair of sweats all week. I didn't run a step because the running made my head hurt. But by Friday, I was feeling fairly well and flew to St. Louis with the team on the day of the game. At our pre-game meal, about four o'clock—the game was a night game to begin at eight—Mike Strofolino, who was supposed to start at outside linebacker in my place kept telling me, "You'd better get ready. I know you're going to start." I said, "Lookit, Mike, I haven't worked out a day during the last week and I haven't run a step in a week." He said, "Now you just remember what I said. I think they're planning on starting you."

After the pre-game meal, I went back to my motel room and lay down, and at six we caught the team bus and went over to the stadium. I was starting to undress when Coach Shroyer called me off to the side. I walked back to the coaches' locker room with him wondering what the hell was happening. I had not expected to play in the game, and I hadn't gotten my psych up; I was figuring to sit on the bench and watch a pretty good football game. Shroyer asked me, "Do you know your defenses?" and I said, "Sure, Don, I know the defenses." He said, "Well listen, I've just talked to Charley and he wants to start you. Are you ready to go?" Many thoughts were racing through my mind, but of course I answered, "Yeah, Don,

I'm ready to go," although I was really pissed off at Winner's decision. Here it was, 6:30 before he decided to inform me I was starting in the ball game at 8:00. Because I hadn't prepared myself mentally, as I normally do, I began to worry about getting it together. The headaches had ceased and I was actually feeling pretty good, but I was worried because I hadn't studied the game plan as thoroughly as I would have if I'd known I was going to start.

We lost and I didn't play very well. The coaches chewed me out and I felt humiliated, but I also felt particularly angry with Winner because he could at least have told me he was thinking about starting me. When I thought about why he would sacrifice me by using me for an exhibition game, I realized he was bowing to pressures from the owners and the St. Louis football fans to try to beat Kansas City and win the Governor's Cup.

Our next to the last exhibition game was played out in San Francisco. I had arranged to get tickets for Chuck Drulis, Jr., and some of his friends, and Chuck had arranged to take care of me in other ways. It was great seeing Chuck and seeing how he freaked out many of the ballplayers because he looked like the archetypal longhair. On the way to the stadium for our pre-game workout the day before the game, Larry Wilson and Irv Goode and Ken Gray kept running from one side of the bus to the other as we were driving by the Golden Gate Panhandle near Haight-Ashbury, hollering and gesturing at the people. "Jesus Christ, look at that one." "Hey, have you ever seen anything like that before?" "Wow, look at that one over there, I'll bet she's a good fuck!" "I can't tell if that's a boy or girl." Rick and I were sitting up in the front of the bus and I turned around and shot a look at them. They were acting like the typical middle-class uptight salesman coming out to San Francisco to see the hippies. I heard the street people in the Haight used to hold up a mirror when the tourist buses would go through to see "the freaks." The message was clear: see who the freaks really are.

26

ON THE RETURN TRIP to St. Louis, I carried with me a half a key of grass, a good quantity of hash, and many tabs of mescaline, psylocibin and acid. Supplies were kind of lean in the midwest and we in St. Louis thought the quality of the stuff would be much better in California. This turned out to be completely true. I was thinking, "Christ, if I get busted now, they'll send me up for a hundred years." But I realized I never would, because I was traveling as one of the straights. Nobody would ever think to finger a professional football player for carrying a load of dope. All through the '69 season I smoked a lot of dope, relaxing after games sitting with friends and blowing a little hash or grass. An increasing number of guys throughout the league are into hash and grass, and a few into psychedelics.

In the Chicago game, the last game of the exhibition season, I tore up my foot on one play. I had defeated the tight end I was playing against, Ray Ogden, and also eliminated the halfback's block. I was going down, ready to make the tackle, when Chuck Walker, the Cardinals' right defensive end drove his man over on my foot. Because my back leg was outstretched, his full weight landed on my heel and tore all the ligaments across the bridge of my foot and ankle. I limped off the field and knew I'd hurt my ankle pretty badly. The following Monday I went to have my ankle x-rayed and I remember thinking as I hobbled in on crutches to see the radiologist, "I hope the goddamned thing is broken." I remember the previous year when the coaches had difficulty relating to my injury because there wasn't tangible evidence for my concussion. My ankle injury precluded this. I would go out on Tuesday in full equipment. The coaches would let me run first team on the right side. I'd stay in for a few plays on pass defense with the first unit and then Shroyer, the linebacker coach, would holler, "Dave, get the hell out of there, you can't run."

But later on, I did go back in before the ankle was healed. I felt I was being cut out, cut off and ignored by the coaching staff and I wanted to contribute in some fashion to the team. Naturally, by doing this every week, I kept re-injuring my ankle. On Tuesday I'd go in, as I did every day, for treatment on my ankle—whirlpool, diathermy, sound and massage. And every day I'd ask Rockwell what he thought my chances were of playing. His comment was, "Well, Dave, you tore it up pretty bad and you know, it just takes time for the ankle to heal. I can't do anything more for you than I am, and you know you can't rush it." We'd gone through this one day in the third week that I was injured when Charley Winner came in, walked over to the whirlpool where I was sitting, and asked Rockwell, "Jack, how is Dave doing?" Rockwell looked at me and I looked at him. He said, "Well, Charley, the ankle is coming along real well." Charley asked him, "Do you think he'll be ready to go this weekend?" and Jack replied, "Well, it looks pretty good, Coach. I think he'll be ready." Charley said, "Well, that's good news," and walked away. I was really confused and pissed off.

Later I cornered Dr. Reynolds, the team physician. I said, "Look, this is ridiculous. You told me my ankle should have been ready a week ago, and Jack told Winner I'd be ready to go. I'm getting to look like a horse's ass, so why don't you shoot my ankle up, and I'll be ready to play." Reynolds explained that my injury was so diffuse he would have to hit me with the needle about ten times to effectively stop the pain; if he did that, my foot would be completely numb, and if I got hit again I could tear up my ankle seriously, and possibly irreparably. Then I was really down. The next Monday I went in and I asked Rockwell, "Jack, do I have a low pain tolerance?" I was really doubting myself. He smiled and said, "No, I don't think you have a particularly low pain tolerance." I asked, "What the fuck's the matter with this ankle?" He said again, "Listen, Dave, you just have to give it time. With that kind of injury it's going to take a while to heal." I decided to get a little intimate with him and said, "This is insane, Jack, why the hell are they having me practice? I go out there every day and run on my ankle and you know it can't be that good for it." He said, "Well, that's probably true. What you should have done is completely sat out the week after it was injured, or even two if necessary. If you would have done that you would have been playing." This really pissed me off, because it was now already into the fifth week, and I hadn't started a regular season game. The most obvious thing would have been to ask Rockwell why he didn't tell the coaches, but I remembered what he'd said to Charley Winner the Friday before.

Bob DeMarco also tore his foot in the same way and on the Friday after his injury, we were sitting in the whirlpool together when Charley Winner came over with Rockwell. For the third time Jack said, "Dave's ankle looks pretty good. He should be ready to go." DeMarco, normally a harsh, outfront New Jerseyan, was an All-Pro center and was one of the mainstays of the Cardinal offensive line. I always thought of him as one guy who would not take shit from the coaches or anybody. I'd heard Rockwell tell DeMarco that his foot was pretty badly injured and that it would be two or three weeks before he was ready. But now, when Charley asked Jack if Bob would be ready on Sunday, Rockwell responded true to form: "His ankle is looking really good coach, and I think he'll be ready to go." After Winner left, DeMarco was outraged. He looked at Rockwell and said, "Godammit, Jack, what'd you tell him that for?" Bob knew that if he didn't play the onus would be on him; it would be a question of his courage, of whether or not he had the guts to play. That Sunday I was walking back in the training room, and there was Bob DeMarco, half-dressed, stretched out on the training room table, gritting his teeth, as Doctor Reynolds shot his ankle and foot full of Novocaine. Even after getting shot up Bob lasted less than half a quarter before he had to come out because of the pain.

During the Minnesota game, Bud Grant had the Vikings line up along the sidelines at attention, holding their helmets under their left arms when the Star Spangled Banner was playing just before the opening kickoff. The Cardinals were, as always, milling around or standing in clumps. When the National Anthem began, we would pop off our helmets and stand in silence. We lost the Minnesota game, and on Monday afternoon, Bob Burns, sports editor of the St. Louis Globe Democrat, came out with a column suggesting one of the reasons for the loss may have been our apparent lack of discipline and order. He noted that the Minnesota players had lined up at attention for the National Anthem while we paid little heed to the flag. Charley Winner saw the piece and Joe Pollack, the PR man, informed him some of the local yahoos were calling in saying that Burns was right. On Wednesday during our general team meeting, Winner said, "Listen, I don't know whether it'll do any good, but it might: next Sunday I want you all to stand along the sidelines, hold your helmets under your left arm, and stand at attention facing the flag while the National Anthem is playing." Charley said the fans also wanted it that way.

The next game all the team members lined up along the sidelines with their helmets under their arms. I'd thought a lot about this and decided that saluting the flag was ridiculous. Every time I even looked at it, I saw only a symbol of repression, so I decided to protest. My original idea was to pull a Tommy Smith by raising my right fist in the air and bowing my head. Instead, I decided not to salute the flag but to pretend I was nervous for the game. I was aware that if my protest was too obvious I would be severely fined. When the National Anthem started I stepped out of line and began kicking the dirt and holding my helmet down in front of me with my two hands. My head was bowed and I was spitting on the ground and moving from side to side scuffing the ground with my shoes.

Bob Burns, the man who wrote the original article,

also had an open line sports show on radio Monday evenings. Joe Pollack, the Cardinal publicist, would rap a while about the game, then the people could call and ask the two of them questions about the previous day's game. That night the shit hit the fan. I didn't hear the program myself, but some of my teammates told me the next day that over half a dozen people had called, all of them outraged at my behavior. Throughout the rest of the season I refused to salute the flag. Before one game, Bob Rowe, the Cardinals' defensive tackle, grabbed me and pulled me in front of himself, directly behind Charley Winner. He said, just screwing around, but within earshot of Winner, "Goddamit Dave, I'm gonna hold you in here and make you salute that flag." When the National Anthem started playing I tried to step out of the line and go through my routine but Rowe had hold of my belt and kept saying fairly loudly, "No, I'm not going to let you step out of this line. You're going to stand in line like the rest of us and salute the flag." All the time he was laughing under his breath.

During the New Orleans game a few weeks later the defense was being mauled. In the fourth quarter I was sitting on the bench completely fagged out when, suddenly, I heard this voice screaming, "Meggyesy! Meggyesy!" I thought it might be a friend trying to attract my attention, so I turned around. There was this irate fan, shaking his fist at me. He had walked down to the edge of the stands and was screaming, "Meggyesy, you goddamn commie, why don't you go to Hanoi?" I smiled and shot him a "V" and then the clenched fist, and I thought the guy was going to have a heart attack. For the remainder of the game, the guy stayed down there and kept on me. At the end of the season, at our last home game, right adjacent to the flagpole was a sign some fans had made up for me with this message: "The Big Red (that was the Cardinals' nickname) Thinks Pink."

We expected to beat Washington in '69. Knowing the material they had and seeing their game films, we expected a fairly easy game. But the game went horribly for us and we lost. Larry Wilson came barging into the locker room following most of the players. I've never seen him so pissed. He was screaming at the coaches and the owners and everybody who wasn't a player, "Get the hell out of here. We want to have a meeting. We want to have a meeting right now." The coaches were freaking, and they all went into a room next to the players' locker room and shut the thin metal door which was all that separated them and the owners who were with them from the players' meeting. Wilson said, "There's something wrong with this ball club. We should never have lost that game today. We're falling apart as a team, and I've called this meeting to hash it out right now." Guys began getting up and airing their gripes about what was going on. It was one of the most intense meetings I've ever been to. One by one the players began to talk about Winner, how he was "chicken-shit" and could not decide on starting personnel or anything else. The majority of the players agreed he was the cause of our miserable season. We all felt there was enough talent in that room to win a championship, yet because of Winner's indecisive handling of things, we were falling apart as a team and not winning. One linebacker got up and said, "I don't care if that motherfucker hears me or not. He's the cause and I don't think there's a man in this room that respects him." Roy Shivers got up and said. "You all know how I feel about the man. I can't play under him, and I think most of you know I'm playing out my option this year." The quarterbacks Johnson and Hart got up and told how they usually didn't know who was going to be the starter until the day before the games. The offensive linemen ran it down about how they had to prepare to use four times as many plays as were necessary so that the offense stagnated during the game. Two resolutions were put forward. One said we knew we were a good football team and we'd have to pull ourselves together by ourselves—that Winner could not be counted on for leadership, so we shouldn't expect it from him. The second one said specifically that the quarterbacks should sit in on all meetings pertaining to the making of the offensive game plans, and that if Winner refused to allow this the players would back the quarterbacks 100 per cent and, if necessary, force the issue into the open.

Winner, his staff and the owners heard everything that was said. But like the black revolt a couple of years before, this meeting was played down and whitewashed. The ownership got tough, which was a typical response. Led by Billy Bidwell, there were suggestions that there were too many fat cats on the Cardinals, and Winner was rehired in 1970. This revolt was undirected and politically naive. But it was, I believe, unprecedented in the National Football League, although the club's attitude was that no real problems existed and that there are always a few malcontents who will bitch at anything.

27

On October 15, as I was going to practice, I was aware of the Moratorium and feeling somewhat guilty for not spending that day working for the end of the war. I didn't quite know what to do. Then on my way to the stadium I passed a group of people handing out petitions for the Businessmen's Committee to End the War in Vietnam. It was a fairly mild statement beseeching the president to end the war as soon as possible and calling for a phased troop withdrawal. As I approached the corner where these people were standing I thought, "Wow, it would be a good idea to have as many ballplayers as possible sign the petition." But then I thought, no, it would do little good. The idea made me somewhat anxious because it meant I would have to confront each person on the squad and ask for his signature, something I didn't particularly want to do. I thought "what the hell," and picked up a bunch of literature and some petitions and took them over to the stadium. I put the literature in each guy's mailbox, got the petition, a clipboard and a pen and began going around the locker room soliciting signatures. Eventually I had 37 signatures out of a possible 50 people. Some of the guys had asked me what the petition was to be used for and I said that it would be sent to President Nixon.

Later that week, I still hadn't sent the petition off, and I showed it to a friend in the advertising business. I told him, "Take a look at this, we might be able to make some use out of it." But I told him not to show it or give it to anybody, because if we were to use it for any publicity purposes I would have to consult with each guy who signed it. About three weeks later this man sent the petition to the head of the Businessmen's Committee to End the War, T. Walter Hardy. T. Walter was out of town and his secretary opened the letter. Realizing the potential of the petition she sent it to another Committee member, a retired advertising man who rewrote the copy, making the statement much stronger, and then released it to the UPI. On the Wednesday before the Detroit game we were ready to go out on the practice field when Charley Winner called us for a special meeting. He read a statement and some notes concerning a conversation he had just had with Stormy Bidwell. He said he wanted to tell everybody this petition was going to be released on the wire services and he didn't want the guys to get upset when they saw it in the papers. After he read the petition, Larry Stallings got up and said, "Whoever is responsible for this should try and get hold of the petition." Since everybody knew I was responsible I got up and said I didn't know how the UPI people had gotten hold of it but I would try to find out. The meeting then broke up and I was going out on the field with the rest of the team when Winner stopped me and said, "Listen, I don't want you to practice today. I want you to get a hold of that petition as soon as you can." So I stripped off my shoulder pads, put on my coat, and—in my football togs, minus shoulder pads and helmet—began calling around trying to find out how the petition had gotten to UPI and who had it. I found out the petition was at T. Walter Hardy's office at Hardy Salt Company in St. Louis and went down to pick it up. His secretary was apologetic and she told me what had happened. The UPI writer had called Joe Pollack, our public relations director, to verify the story. Pollack pleaded with the guy to hold it up and called Stormy Bidwell in Chicago. Stormy was slightly outraged and called Winner. After I got the petition I called Stormy in Chicago and explained what had happened.

The next day I felt that I had to appear before the squad, even though I was quite embarrassed because it seemed I'd betrayed their confidence. I got up and explained what had happened. In closing, I told them that I still felt they could do something in the form of a letter or petition protesting the war in Vietnam, and that anybody who was interested could get in touch with me after practice. As I was saying this I noticed Winner's jaw tightening and he really looked pissed. He got up after I was through and mumbled something about how he appreciated my talking to the squad and then said, "Anybody who is involved in further political organizing will be dealt with by the head coach."

I started the Detroit game that week and played fairly well. With my injury healed, I was beginning to hit the groove and looked forward to finishing strong the last part of the season. My brother Dennis was visiting me, and we talked all night long: about football and all the bullshit related to it, the authoritarian coaches, the stupid rules, the paternalistic attitudes and how the glorification and exhibition of individual and collective violence was a royal bummer. I was really feeling good because I was understanding so much more about myself and about what I was doing than ever before.

The next Sunday we were to play Philadelphia in St. Louis. That Monday, I got a call from Sandy Padwe, a sportswriter for the Philadelphia Inquirer. After talking a few minutes with Sandy, I decided he was a man I could trust so I told him exactly what I was thinking about myself and football and how I saw football in the context of society. I said, "When society changes in the way I hope it will, football will be obsolete." I talked about the militarism of the game and how football is middle America's theater.

During our kicking game workout on Saturday morning before the Philadelphia game, I began having intense chest pains. I could barely stand up. After practice I went in and told Rockwell my problem and he called the team physician, Dr. Newton. Newton suggested I go home and rest because I probably had some form of pleurisy. I went home and got in bed immediately. My fever spiked about ten that night at 105° and by four the next morning it finally broke. The 24-hour flu had really jumped on my back, but I went down for the game around 10:30 in the morning and saw Dr. Newton. He asked me how I was feeling, and I told him I was ready to play but feeling weak. He wanted to consult with the coaches and tell them exactly how I was feeling, and let them decide whether I should start or not. As he was walking out of the training room I told him to make sure he said I was ready to go— "I'm just a little weak, but I could take a couple of bennies to get myself up." He went and talked to the coaches and as I was getting dressed, Don Shroyer, the linebacker coach, came over and asked me how I was feeling. I told him what I had told the doctor and he said, "O.K., we want you to sit out and we'll start Rosema." Rosema started and played an average game. The next Tuesday we went out after the films for our traditional light workout. I lined up in my regular right linebacker's position. Shroyer hollered to Rosema, "Rocky, get in there." It was very clear that he meant get in there for Meggyesy, though he didn't use my name. I walked to the sideline wondering what the hell happened, why I was being demoted. Interestingly, Shroyer did not speak one word to me during the remainder of the season. By the time practice ended I was fuming. As Chuck Drulis was coming in the door I stood up and told him I wanted to talk to him. We moved over to the side of the room and I asked him, "Why have I been put down?" He answered, "You have?" and I said "Yes, didn't you see practice today? Rocky was playing Number 1." He said, "Well, I didn't know you were moved but sometimes we move people around, I wouldn't worry about it." I was still pretty pissed and felt he was trying to give me the runaround. I said, "Listen, are you the head defensive coach?" He said "Yes, but . . ." And I said, "But nothing, Chuck, I've been moved down." He said "Honest, Dave, I really don't know anything about it. I'll check with the head man and talk with you tomorrow." At that point, for some strange reason, I really believed Chuck didn't know anything about it.

The next morning I saw Chuck in the hallway leading to the Cardinal offices. He ducked his head in to escape me, and I had to run after him and call his name. He turned around and I said, "Well, have you checked?" He said, "Yes, I have talked with Winner and we want to start the other guy for a while." I'd thought it through the night before and realized I was getting the shaft. I grunted, "Thanks a lot Chuck," and went down to the locker room.

That day after practice I confronted Charley Winner as he was coming in the locker room. We moved off to the side and I said, "Why have you put me down?" He said, "Dave, as I told everybody in training camp, I don't have to tell anybody why I move them." I said, "Charley, you may think you can tell that kind of story to some rookie, but I've been playing in this league for seven years and I think I deserve an explanation." Surprised, he said, "Well, we felt that you made a lot of mistakes in Detroit and we wanted to start Rosema." I was on the verge of screaming at him or punching him out, but I said nothing and he simply walked away. I was demoted to the bomb squad but I decided I wasn't about to go down and be a maniac on the kickoff team and managed not to get knocked off my feet for the rest of the season.

About two weeks later, Bob Rowe was goading Jack Rockwell, an extreme right-winger, by asking him what he thought about the My Lai massacres. Rick Sortun was up on the training table getting taped and I was standing alongside. Jack said some lame thing about the fortunes of war and Rick hit the bait—which was what Rowe wanted. He started blowing away on Rockwell and I too chimed in. Suddenly Jack stopped taping Rick's ankle. He looked up at me and said, "Dave, I have listened to you for five years. Though I haven't believed what you said, I have at least respected your arguments." By this time his voice was raising to a shout and he said, "But what you said in the Philadelphia newspapers, I could never buy." The whole scene flashed in front of me and I started to laugh. I said, "Did the coaches see the Philadelphia newspaper by any chance?" and he said, "Of course, we get all the papers from the NFL cities." It was now very clear. The coaches hadn't seen Sandy's article until after the Philadelphia game and were obviously outraged by my comments and decided to demote me.

The last part of the season was almost a nightmare. I showed up every day for practice, but I was completely ostracized by the coaching staff. Winner, Shroyer, Voris and Drulis did not speak a total of five words to me after reading the interview. I was just going through the motions running down on the bomb squads. After our last game of the season, when we played the Green Bay Packers, I was talking with Larry Stallings. He said "Dave, I don't know what went on between you and the coaches and I don't want to know, but your not being in there sure hurt our defense."

After the season I broke loose like a free man. I flew out to the West Coast and visited Chuck Drulis, Jr. down in Ken Kesey's old haunt at La Honda and dropped some righteous sunshine acid.

About four days after I'd returned to St. Louis from my trip to California, I got a call from Jack Scott, who was teaching a course on athletics and American life at the University of California at Berkeley. Sandy Padwe, who is a close friend of Jack's, had told him about my ideas and had also sent me a copy of Jack's book, *Athletics for Athletes,* so we more or less knew each other, although we hadn't met. Jack asked me to come out and be a guest lecturer for his course, and I agreed. The week in the Bay Area that followed was one of the most intense in my life. It went beautifully. I discovered that Jack and I had very similar backgrounds in sports and that he too had gone through the Syracuse athletic mill, though a few years after me.

I lived with Jack and his wife, Micki, the week I was in California rapping with the Berkeley students. In talking with the Cal football players enrolled in Jack's course, I discovered that though Rick Sortun and I were rarities in pro ball, many college ball players were much further along the road of becoming athletes in revolt than Rick and I were during our college years.

By the time I went home, I knew what had to be done. I sold my house in St. Louis and most of my furniture Then Stacy and I loaded up the kids, a few belongings, and my dog Sam, and drove back out to Berkeley. It had taken a long time, but I had finally made the break.

Now that football and the split personality it forced on me were part of the past, I knew I could get down to the real work—joining forces with those individuals and groups trying to change this society.

Acknowledgements

WRITING THIS BOOK was a new and difficult experience. I am indebted to the Institute for the Study of Sport and Society, and particularly to its Director, Jack Scott. Jack worked closely and tirelessly with me roughly eight hours a day for five months to help put my ideas in readable form. Although the responsibility for the ideas and thoughts set down here is mine, Jack's vision in seeing the need for the book and his unceasing devotion to this vision made the final manuscript possible. The facilities made available to me at the Institute and the assistance of staff researcher Micki Scott made possible uninterrupted work and thought in a time of hectic personal change.

To Peter Collier at Ramparts Press, who in January saw the importance of this book, I owe a debt of thanks. Without his invaluable editorial assistance, particularly in the latter stages of the manuscript's preparation, publication of the book would have been delayed many months.

Dave Burgin, Executive Sports Editor of the San Francisco *Examiner*, and John Clancy offered important criticisms and suggestions as the work was in progress. Phil

Finch's sensitive and accurate report of the reasons for my retirement in the *Examiner* (and the generally positive response to his piece) reaffirmed my belief in the possible significance the book would have in the sports world.

Lastly, I would like to thank those who were instrumental in the actual construction of the book, particularly Marta Kaldenbach, who had the thankless and difficult job of typing taped transcripts in the initial stages of the work. Peter Solomon, Editor of Ramparts Press, and Judy Hirsch devoted much time to rereading, editing and checking the myriad details involved in making a book.

During the course of my fourteen years playing football many people shared ideas and thoughts with me which were important in shaping my own thinking about football and my relation to the game. Quitting the game at the height of my career was one product of an on-going process of personal growth and intellectual development. These particular individuals, among many, were integral parts of that process: Bill and Sally Davidson, Bill Davidson, Jr., Coach Bob Vogt, Professor Roger Milkman, Allen Green, Gene Stancin, Hank Woessner, John Hartwell Moore, Dr. Bruce Heyl, Marty Lebowitz, Stormy Bidwell, Professor Irving Louis Horowitz, Rick Sortun, Dr. John Schengber, Dennis Meggyesy, Seymour Carter, Professor Herbert Blumer, Professor Ernest Becker, Sandy Padwe, John and Pamela Clancy, and Jack Scott. Also there are those people whose ideas and actions have begun to make the revolution possible: the Black college athletes who have exposed, by their protests, the racism in organized sport, particularly Harry Edwards and Tommie Smith; John Sinclair, Chairman of the White Panthers, Bobby

Seale, Chairman of the Black Panther Party; and others who have given their hearts, minds and lives to radically transform this country to enable the creation of a just, humane society.

Finally, to Stacy Meggyesy, whose love, understanding and concern were a constant source of strength during most of my years as a football player and especially during the intense and many times painful period while this book was being written—thank you.

Dave Meggyesy wrote this book over a six-month period while at the Institute for the Study of Sport and Society. The Institute was founded in Oakland, California, during the spring of 1970 with one of its chief purposes being to examine the role of sports in American society.

Out of Their League is the first book to be written by an athlete working at the Institute. In our opinion, this book sets a new standard for sport autobiographies, and we are proud to have been associated with its development. My own contribution to the book was greatly aided by advice and suggestions I received from many individuals while the work was in progress, but I would especially like to thank Dave Burgin, Sandy Padwe, and Leonard Shecter.

Jack Scott
Director
Institute for the Study of Sport and Society